Lovebirds

All About Nutrition, Training
Care, Diseases and Treatments

Copyright © 2016 Erika Busecan

ISBN-13:978-1540371812

ISBN-10:1540371816

Contents

Lovebirds

Lovebirds are one of the most widely kept and most popular parrots among other birds.

Lovebirds are very beautiful exotic birds and belong to the Psittacidae family of the genus Agapornis. There are nine species of Lovebirds: the grey-headed Lovebird is originally from Madagascar and the other eight species are native to the African continent. Lovebirds are small parrots in comparison with other parrot species, they are also been called "pocket parrots". In the United States the most commonly kept species are the Peach-faced Lovebird (Agapornis Roseicollis Roseicollis), the Black-masked (Agapornis Personata Personata) and the Fischer's Lovebird (Agapornis Personata Fischeri).

In the wild, Lovebirds are very noisy birds and live in small flocks, in arid inland areas, savannas and farmlands. In some areas, many wild Lovebirds may be killed for the damages they produce to agriculture crops, but in other regions they are protected by law. These extraordinary birds mate for life, but if the mate dies, the companion usually will remate soon. In the wild, Lovebirds build their nest in tree hollows, in rocks or in shrubs. Lovebirds migrates irregularly from place to place in search of water and food.

The nine species of Lovebirds are: Peach-faced Lovebird (Agapornis Roseicollis), Fischer's Lovebird (Agapornis Fischeri), Black-Cheeked Lovebird (Agapornis Nigrigenis), Yellow-Collared Lovebird or Black-Masked Lovebird (Agapornis Personatus), Black-Collared or Swindern's Lovebird (Agapornis Swindernianus), or Abyssinian Lovebird (Agapornis Taranta), Grey-Headed Lovebird or Madagascar Lovebird (Agapornis Canus), Red- Headed Lovebird or Red- Faced Lovebird (Agapornis Pullarius) and Lilian's Lovebird or Nyasa Lovebird (Agapornis Lilianae).

Peach-faced Lovebird

Presents mostly green plumage with bright red- peach head and throat, yellow coloration of the belly, blue, red and green tail feathers.

Peach-Faced Lovebirds have beige color beak and they have no eye ring.

Fischer's Lovebird

Presents mostly green plumage with dark green feathers on the wings and the back, orange head and upper body, blue lower back, rump and tail.

Fischer's Lovebird has prominent white eye ring and red beak.

Black-Cheeked Lovebird

Presents mostly green plumage, dark brown cheeks and throat, reddish-brown forehead and orange chest, yellow-olive feathers on the nape.

Black-cheeked Lovebirds have prominent white eye ring and red beak.

Yellow-Collared Lovebird

Presents mostly green plumage with yellow upper body, dark sooty brown cheeks and head and grayish-blue tail feathers.

Yellow-Collared Lovebirds have prominent white eye ring and red beak. The female is slightly bigger than the male.

Black-Winged Lovebird

Presents mostly green plumage with black wing feathers and red beak.

These birds have no eye ring, are sexually dimorphic, which means that only the male has red feathers on the crown, around the eyes and on the forehead. The female`s plumage is all green without any red coloration on the head.

Grey-Headed Lovebird

Presents mostly green plumage with dark grey on the back, pale grey upper body, neck, head and the beak is light grey in color.

These birds have no eye ring, are sexually dimorphic, which means that the male has grey upper body, neck and head. The females are fully green colored.

Red-Headed Lovebird

Presents mostly green plumage with some yellow feathers on the chest and on the underwings, red face and red beak.

These birds have no eye ring, are sexually dimorphic,

which means that the male has a darker red face and beak than the female.

Lilian's Lovebird

Presents mostly green plumage with darker green on the back and the rump area, orange head and upper chest, red beak and prominent white eye ring.

Description

The Lovebird is one of the smallest bird in the parrots family. Lovebirds have stocky bodies, short tails, large hooked bills and specific feet: two toes pointing forward and two pointing backward. The beak is large in comparison with their body. Depending on the species, wild Lovebirds plumage is usually green with various colors on their upper bodies. Lovebirds mate for life, remaining close to one another and regularly preening and feeding each other. If the mate dies, the companion usually will remate soon. Young Lovebirds have black lines on their beaks up to 8 weeks old.

The Lovebird`s body length is between 13-18cm (5-7 inches) from beak to the tip of the tail feathers and weighs around 40-70 grams (0.088 - 0.154 pounds).

Areas of a Lovebird

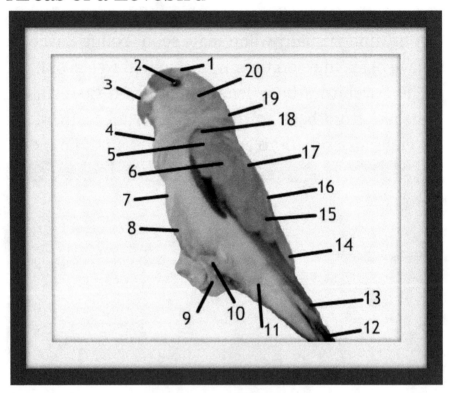

1. Crown
2. Eye
3. Beak
4. Throat
5. Lesser wing coverts
6. Median wing coverts
7. Breast
8. Abdomen
9. Toe
10. Leg
11. Vent
12. Tail
13. Primary feathers
14. Secondary feathers
15. Secondary coverts
16. Scapulars
17. Mantle
18. Band of wing
19. Nape
20. Ear coverts

Character

Lovebirds are very curious, active, playful and full of affection birds. Lovebirds have the abilities and the intelligence of some of the larger parrots.

Lovebirds do not have to be kept in pairs to have happy lives, they are like many other species of parrots and they can be kept as single birds or in bonded pairs. If their mate dies, they will usually bond with other Lovebird.

Lovebirds are territorial and can be aggressive especially during mating season, when they may become hormonal and jealous. Interactions between Lovebirds and other pets like cats or dogs should be supervised, because these birds can be mean. They should not be kept together with smaller birds, because they may bite off the toes of other birds. Parrots that were previously captured in the wild have an extraordinary repertoire of whistling sounds and they sing and whistle very often during the nights, especially in those with full moon. In the wild the male use specific sounds to attract the female.

Lovebirds are more talented in whistling than they are at talking and they rarely talk or mimic human speech. The female Lovebird is more affectionate and usually in breeding season she is more protective of its cage and nest than the male.

They are not considered to be too noisy birds in

comparison with other parrots species, using chirping and screeching sounds. Lovebirds are very social birds and they will happily sit on your finger or shoulder. A single bird will need a lot of interaction with the owner. Lovebirds may bite if frightened by sudden hand movements, so they don't make good pets for everyone.

They need a lot of toys and a very strong relationship with humans to prevent behavioral problems.

Older birds are less adaptable to a new owner and they will react by tearing their feathers in response to this kind of changes in their life. Young parrots can adapt very easy to new environments.

Lovebirds are very sociable birds, but when they are neglected might become depressed, they may pull their feathers and refuse to eat. Lovebirds love to play very often and they are getting bored very easy. To keep them happy, all you need to do is to make sure that there are toys (plastic chains, perches, swings, ladders), pieces of wood (from which they can nibble) and tree branches available for them. In the wild, if a member of a flock will learn a new skill, then the other members will copy that new skill, because it plays an important role in their survival. Wild parrots have to be always ready to protect their territory, to find food and water, to avoid raptors, to defend their pair and to transmit these qualities to their descendants.

So if you decide to bring a parrot as a pet in your house, you'll have to know that you will need to dedicate time, patience and affection, every single day to your bird.

Your parrot will need to learn to cooperate, to tolerate environmental changes and to accept veterinary care and examinations. S/he has to develop a strong sense of its own personality, otherwise if a bird doesn't learn to clean itself or to play when s/he is alone, after all s/he will decide that the owner can satisfy every kind of their necessity. You'll have to guide your bird towards an acceptable behavior, because it's much easier to prevent bad behaviors, rather than change them.

Because in the wild, parrots used to live in holes of trees, it`s very important to offer them wood sticks to chew. Parrots usually represent a very long term responsibility and they are not the perfect choice for everyone. Some owners often frighten sensitive Lovebirds with their sudden movements, by putting a new toy in their cage or by trying to hand them to strangers. Chasing a sensitive and frightened bird and trying to catch it and comfort it, is the last thing we want to do. This is the perfect example of how our bird will lose confidence in us.

In these situations, the best thing is to leave the bird

alone until it has calmed down.

If your parrot starts screaming for attention and you scream back at the bird, then what you have done, is that you reinforced the bad behavior of the bird. Screaming out of boredom is another common situation among Lovebirds. To stop excessive screaming, first you need to change your interaction with your bird, then try to get a bigger cage, add more natural branches and wood to chew on, replace the old toys with new ones as frequently as possible. If by mistake, you taught your bird that it will get your attention when it screams, then you must stop giving it any attention and give it attention when it is quiet and behaving nicely.

Some people think that their bird will bite them. The bird won't bite you as long as you try to manipulate the bird by using your hands and fingers in a friendly and calm way.

People use to react when the bird wants to step up on their finger by grabbing the finger with their beak and people think that the bird it's going to bite and they pull their finger away, but all s/he wants is to step up on your finger, because s/he thinks it`s a branch of a tree. If you pull your finger away, it`s going to grab and hold your finger with her/his beak and you will reinforce the bird for another bad habit and s/he will realise, that if s/he grab your finger, it will cause another reaction, another drama.

So you have to use positive reinforcement for behavior not resulting in biting. Don't forget, they do have the potential to become very cuddly and devoted birds, and they tend to become attached to their owners.

Youngsters should be socialised to many people and exposed to a variety of situations such as handling by friends, visits to the veterinarian, nail and wing clipping, to avoid fear of new situations. Young Lovebirds that grow up near other adult Lovebirds, are less likely to be emotionally unstable, because they are capable to study and learn the more experienced birds behaviour.

Getting to know someone that has experience in raising Lovebirds will help you decide, if they are the right birds for you.

Parrots can produce a powder like substance, which helps them to clean and to protect their feathers, but it may cause allergies to humans.

Life span

In captivity birds can live much longer than their wild relatives with the condition that they get all the necessary nutrition and care which they need. Even in captivity, the lack of food, incomplete diet and improper care of parrots could lead to a considerably shorter life span.

The Lovebird`s life span is between 15-20 years.

How to choose the right bird

General criteria

Parrots are very lovely exotic birds, so if you want to be happy with your bird, you have to study your parrot species personality and abilities, which will help to create a perfect pet-owner relationship, leading to a happy life together.

If you ask a few people who wish to have an exotic bird about what they are expecting from the bird, the answer will be: to be smart, to be beautiful, to be able to learn to speak as fast as possible, to have a perfect singing voice, to be a clean bird, without damaging things in the house and the cost for everyday needs of the bird to be as cheap as possible. Before you make a decision to purchase a bird, you have to be aware of the fact that very few birds could match your expectations and you have to realise that these birds will be your companions for many years.

A parrot requires less time than a dog and it`s easy to maintain, but don't forget that it will need food, cage cleaning and at least once a day fresh water.

Your birds need your companionship and affection and it`s very important to spend few moments daily with them.

If you are uncertain about keeping a pair or just a single parrot, then you have to take into consideration that a single bird is much easier to maintain and to train. But if you don't have enough time to spend with him/her every single day, then I would strongly recommend to buy a pair instead of a single bird.

If you decide to purchase a single bird, but you are uncertain about the bird's gender, then you have to take into consideration that the males are ideal pet birds and can be easier domesticated than females. Males are not as noisy and destructive as females during breeding season and they can learn much easier to speak, because of their capacity for imitation. Another personal advice: take the bird with you if you are going in holiday, because they just love going in holiday and love spend all their time with you and your family.

How to purchase a healthy bird

Purchasing a bird directly from the breeder or from the pet store has multiple advantages. You can get information about their health condition, their provenience and also you can check the quality of the environment where they've been kept. You have to know a few aspects which could indicate hidden diseases: the bird has to be active with a good stability on its feet; the nostrils must be clean without secretion; the feathers around the beak must be clean; the bird`s breathe has to be clear without whistling sounds; the eyes have to be clear; the missing feathers from the wings or tail could indicate "french moulting"- viral disease which leads to feathers loss; dirty feathers (with feces) at the vent area could indicate digestive system problems.

How to determine the parrot`s gender

With some exceptions, parrots are sexually monomorphic, which means that their gender can`t be determined by their markings or the color of their feathers. Differences of the appearance between the two genders are very small and you can`t recognize the gender of the bird by looking at it. In Lovebirds, the color of some males may appear more vibrant than the females. The female is more rounded-bodied and a little bit smaller than the male, and the female`s tail appear more square, while the male`s appear more rounded. However, there can be behavioral clues once these birds reach 1 year of age, the male may regurgitate in the presence of the owner (which is how they feed a nesting female) while the female will shred and stuff the paper strips into her feathers, doing more work than the male.

The easiest and less expensive method for determining a parrot`s gender is through quick DNA testing. There are lots of companies offering DNA testing as a mail-order service. You need some fresh cells of your bird, so DNA can be extracted from them. You can get some cells of your bird by carefully plucking off 2-4 feathers from the chest of the bird.

This is a little bit painful for the bird, but does not have any long term effects. Feathers that are shed naturally, are not suitable for extracting DNA (they lack blood and live cells). The pulled out feathers can be send to a specialized laboratory that offers sexing of birds.

Life with cage birds

Preparing your house for the new arrived parrot

Before you bring your beloved bird in your house, first you have to find a proper place for it. It means that this place has to be quiet and without any air currents. The cage has to be equipped with all the necessary things: food, water and toys.

First day it`s better to offer a little bit of privacy to the bird, even if we like to watch it, and it is recommended to cover the cage, especially during the day. If you already own birds, the new arrived bird has to be isolated in a separate cage (cages which are usually used for the transportation of the bird). You have to leave the bird to get used with the new conditions and with you, the new owner.

A parrot is considered accommodate when it doesn't get scared at the appearance of the owner, when s/he is feeding properly and when its feathers look normal. After the accommodation process, when you want to move your bird in another cage with the other birds, instead of stressing the bird by catching it with your hands, you better bring closer the entrances of the two cages and leave them in this position for a while, to give the chance to your bird to get into the other cage whenever s/he wants and when it is totally relaxed.

The transportation of the parrots

Transportation of the birds can be dangerous when it's done improperly and can cause serious problems to your bird.

When you transport your bird from your vet or from pet shop to your home it is recommended to keep it in a special cage without water and food bowls in it, or in special carton boxes with tiny holes in them for the bird to be able to breath and to avoid accidents.

If you choose the cage, you better cover it with a piece of thin, dark colored material and make sure that it has a hole on the top for the holder of the cage.

You can also transport your bird in a bigger shoe box with lid. The box must present on the sides little holes that you can handmade them which are necessary for the air circulation inside the box.

The new arrived parrot's diet

When you purchase your bird, you have to know all about your bird's diet: what kind of food s/he has previously consumed. If the bird has not received the proper diet, then you have to replace it gradually. You'll need to offer your new arrived bird, freshwater and pieces of apple. If your bird presents signs of weakness, you'll have to offer some moist biscuits and egg paste; if s/he looks healthy, you can give your bird the usual food, but also you can add in his/her food some poppy seeds (it will have a calming effect on your bird). The chamomile tea (instead of water) has also a good calming effect and makes your bird to feel more relaxed.

How to train your parrot

Talking and training

The best time to start training a Lovebird is at the age of 7-10 months old. The right owner for a Lovebird has to be somebody who want to invest time in it, and for this reason, before you get a parrot, you have to study these birds behavior and learn about what are the requirements to look after them. The most important thing that you have to do is getting your bird used with other people. You have to make sure that almost every day your parrot will have the chance to get in contact with new people, to experience new surroundings. All those experiences and interactions with other people must be a positive experience for him/her.

Lovebirds do have the ability to mimic human speech even though they are not among those birds that would consider to be talking parrots.

Don't forget that a handfed Lovebird is more likely to talk, than the one reared by the parents.

If you really want to teach your parrot to talk, then you'll have to be more patient, you'll have to speak very often with him/her, and your voice has to be very calm. The training lessons have to represent positive experiences for your parrot and they have to last for about 5-10 minutes, once or twice a day. It could be one hour after the bird wakes up and about one hour before the bird goes to sleep, that`s because during daytime the bird is most active and when they are active they`are less inclined to be open to training. You have to combine training time with play time, because you actually want to make the bird to enjoy the training because they deal with a positive experience.

You'll have to encourage your parrot with the right words like "well done" and you'll have to offer rewards every time s/he will say the words right.

Be aware, never yell or hurt your parrot when s/he is doing something wrong or you feel that s/he is stressing you. The bird will lose its confidence in you and will be very hard for you to regain it again. For the first days, don't try to handle the bird, because the most important thing is to get used with each other.

Place the cage in the same room where you use to spend most time. Talk to your bird as much as possible and when you change the water and food, try to do it by not stressing the bird too much. Offer your bird small treats, when it seems fine with you being there. After a few days you can leave the cage door open and hold out a treat, so encouraging your bird to come sit on the cage door. Place some food in your hand and encourage the bird to eat from your palm. Your bird will realise that you are its best friend and s/he will come out of the cage and will learn to step up on your finger. Soon you will observe that your parrot will sit very comfortable on your shoulder, which means that s/he accepted you.

Parrots, in general, love sitting on people's shoulders and love to chew things which decreases their aggression and actual depression problems. They like to chew on your hair, you don't have to worry about it (they don't bite it off), they're just chewing on it because they're enjoying that.

One of the most important word for your parrot to learn is "step up". Even if s/he steps up on your finger without any previous command, it is recommended to say the words "step up" every time the bird is performing your command and you'll have to say: "well done", "good girl" or "good boy" after that.

Some parrots do learn to talk very well, but first they learn to talk on their own, by listening human conversations and imitating sounds. So, the first thing you can do to encourage your parrot to talk, is to repeat the words all the time. To encourage your parrot to say specific phrases that you really want your parrot to repeat, try to say them in a regular basis. Talk to your parrot when s/he is concentrated at you, that is usually when his/her eyes are attentive. The first word that most parrot will learn is "Hello", because that is the first thing they hear whenever someone walks into a room.

It`s very important to reward and to answer to your parrot every time it`s saying words or making sounds, even if they are correct or not. Don't scream at your bird when s/he is very loud, you better try to maintain a calm conversation. Watch out what you say in front of your bird, parrots use to learn much quicker the words that you don't really want them to learn.

You can use clickers with success to achieve the best training results. Parrots usually learn quicker when you're using a clicker. When you start training your bird, first give it a treat and in the same time say "well done" or click the clicker. Your parrot will associate these sounds with the treat. Once the bird makes the association between praise (click) and treat, you can delay the reward. If your parrot already knows the "step up" command, then it`s easy to teach him/her to say "hello". You'll have to raise your hand in front of the bird, just like you want the bird to step up on it. When s/he steps up say "well done" and give your bird the treat. Repeat this command for a few times, until the bird will understand it. Once the bird has raised his/her leg on its own to get the treat, wait and give the treat only when the bird is raising its leg a little bit higher. You can also use very subtle signs with your hands if you want your parrot to answer back to you. You have to choose a sign and use it in the same way you use a command, followed by a treat or a praise. Your bird will learn very fast every little movements of your fingers.

Teach your parrot to play basketball, using a miniature - sized basketball hoop by picking up "an easy to hold ball" and passing it through the tiny basket. Show your bird the basketball and say "Toss!" and then put the basketball through the hoop. Next, hand the ball to your bird and say "Toss!" If your bird puts the ball through the hoop, say "Well done!" in a happy, excited tone.

Rope climbing exercise:

For this exercise you will need a cotton rope (about 2.5-3 meters long), make knots on it about every 15 cm. Attach the rope from the ceiling using a metal hook. Place the parrot on the floor at the end of the rope and say, "Climb the rope!"

If your parrot doesn't want to climb upward on the rope, then you will have to hold a treat at 20 cm above the bird, and gradually move the treat towards the top end of the rope. As soon as your bird gets to the top knot, say, "Well done!" and at the same time give it the treat. You can repeat this exercise 5-6 times in one session. If your parrot already knows how to perform the exercise, you can replace the treats with lots of encouraging words.

How to train parrots to stop biting

When parrots feel threatened they will react in different ways, like screaming, flapping their wings, running away, hissing, biting, etc...

There are several factors that can make parrots feel threatened like, perturbing them when attention is not wanted, invading their territory, sudden movements, unexpected noises, jealousy.

Parrots can also bite when protecting their mate. In captivity your parrot will bond with you, so if your bird has chosen you for a mate, it may feel that unfamiliar persons or new pets appear as a threat to your safety.

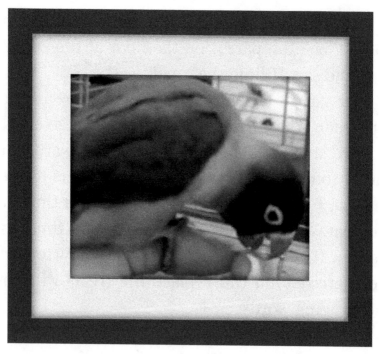

In these situations it is best to gradually introduce your bird to the new person or pet, allowing your bird enough time to accept the change.

Parrots who are going through hormonal changes during the breeding season or molting may become annoyed and moody which may lead to biting. You should watch your bird body language during these periods and leave your bird alone when attention is not wanted. It`s our natural behavior when a bird bites, to put the bird down and then we start to yell at that bird. In this situation we reinforce the bird to bite us, because that brings the bird more and more attention.

When your young parrot try to nibble on your ears,

fingers or other body parts you should offer them an acceptable alternative to chew on: apple slice, carrot, block of wood, etc... If the method above doesn't work, then gently blow in their face and in a firm voice tell them "no".

All we want to do is to reinforce and reward good behaviors like doing interactive things, standing on your hand, playing quietly, that are positive and socially acceptable.

For example, choose a toy, a key or an object which could interest your parrot, when s/he is touching that object reward or praise your bird. After s/he seems to look that s/he understand that command, make it to pick up that object. You have to repeat this game until your parrot will pick it up and will bring you that object.

Training lessons have to be short about 5-10 minutes and to represent a positive experience for you and for your bird.

The rewards (treats) have to be small quantities, but also something that your bird will enjoy to eat, like sunflower seeds, for example. If you offer big rewards to your bird, then s/he will spend too much time to eat them and your training lesson will be interrupted for too long.

If your bird bites you, try hard not to even yell out in pain, just take the bird, put it down and walk away.

Your parrot will learn, that when s/he bites you, then s/he will lose your attention.

Make sure your bird have things available to play with, so that s/he will not bite you. Your parrot can`t eat and bite, can't shred toys and bite at the same time, so if you can anticipate the behavior from happening, regardless of what the behavior is (biting, screaming) and you can provide some sort of distraction for your bird, they will not bite.

You can place a wooden chopstick within the bird`s rich. When the bird does bite the stick, you should praise it. After all, your bird will understand that biting a stick is a good thing.

Learn to observe your parrot's body language

Parrots usually show us how they're feeling and what they're going to do, by using their bodies in different ways, because they tend to communicate with us this way.

When they have their tail flared it means that they are excited or they will bite you. If your parrot has all its feathers sticking out, with it's wings held out from the body, then s/he could be ready to fight.

You can also observe a few clues at your parrot, when s/he intend to bite. It will open its beak and will spread its legs apart for a firmer grip on the perch.

You can interact with your parrot to prevent the bite, when you observe these kind of signs.

When your parrot is happy to see a friend of yours or another bird, then s/he might puff out all its feathers or wag its tail or moves its beak up and down, stretch one wing and one leg together out from the side of the body.

When your Lovebird gets very small, it could mean that it is scared.

Cold season, hot season

How to care of your bird in cold season

Exotic birds can't resist at sudden weather changes (from sudden cold to sudden hot weather), you'll have to maintain a constant temperature for them during winter. Parrots like humidity, so if the air condition of your house is very dry, because of the heating system, it is recommended to spray your bird daily with a handheld spray bottle.

How to care of your bird in hot season

Many people think that parrots feel at "home" in high temperatures, but bird owners have to be prepared for hot weather. Bird's body temperature is between 104-105.8 degrees Fahrenheit (40-41 degrees Celsius), therefore your bird will withstand temperatures that goes up until this level. Birds don't have sweat glands like we do, so they can't adjust their body temperature. When we perspire, the evaporation of the moisture on our skin cools us. There are several ways in which your bird can drop his own body temperature:

- heat loss during panting: birds increase their breathing rate, by faster breathing with the beak open. They have dry mouths and while we see them panting, when they're overheated, they're reacting to the heat and this does not means that they can combat it without our help. Their life could be in danger, because they can become dehydrated by evaporation of the water through respiratory system (mouth, nostrils and lungs).

- evaporation of water through skin and feet
- through vibration of the neck structures.

Birds that are brought outside should be watched closely. If you observe that your parrot is holding its wings away from its body and is panting, then you have to bring it to cooler temperatures and give it a shower with water at room temperature. Using cold water on overheated bird can cause organ damage, shock and even death.

Don't place the cage in direct sunlight, because your bird will need a shady place and humidity. You can attach a spray or sprinkler system to the top of the cage or of your aviary and you can also set a timer on, and cool down the cages to offer your bird a refreshing shower.

Cages and accessories

When you choose a cage for your bird you have to take into consideration the size and the temperament of your bird, because s/he will spend almost all it`s time in that cage.

You have to assure your bird with the ability to fly without any problem between the climbing perches or to flap its wings.

Cage location

Your parrot just adore you to be around him/her, so you'll have to place the cage in the same room where you spend most of your time.

To avoid any possible danger, you'll have to take into consideration a few aspects:

- place the cage near the window, so your parrot can enjoy the natural light;
- avoid placing the cage in air currents;
- avoid placing the cage in the kitchen, especially when you cook, because the steam could contain toxic substances for your parrot;
- don't place the cage near television or near any home audio system;

Cages

The cage has to be two or three times bigger than the bird's wingspan and three times bigger than the bird's length from head to tail. It has to be big enough for the bird, so it will be able to open its wings and flaps them.

The minimum size of the cage should be at 18 inches (45.72 cm) tall, 18 inches (45.72 cm) in width and 22 inches (55.88 cm) in depth. Especially for single birds you'll have to equip the cage with lots of toys, mirrors and swings. You'll have to change the toys very often, to keep your bird from becoming bored.

To maintain your parrot's feet health, you must provide proper perches for the bird, otherwise it will be difficult for your parrot to properly hold on to a perch.

Your parrot should be able to stand on the perch, without the toes completely touching each other in a circle.

If you choose to offer your parrot natural branch perches, make sure that they are without any wild bird droppings and free of insects. You'll have to disinfect it with hot boiled water, before using it.

There are lots of great perches on the market now like sandy perches, calcium perches and mineral perches for chewing to provide essential minerals and for keeping nails and beaks trimmed.

These perches are great to use beside your basic perches. Sandy perches should be positioned near feeding pots (fruit, veggie or sticky food) as your parrot will use the perch to wipe his/her beak during eating.

There are also comfortable braided rope perches, which are good choice for your birds as they are natural climbers and swingers so fully enjoy the use of ropes.

The resistance of the cage is very important, one made of metal is much resistant than one made of plastic. The space between the bars it`s very important (it should be around ½ inch apart, because the bird could get it's head, legs or even its beak stuck. When you buy a cage make sure that it's not painted, because parrots will eat the paint, and if the paint is toxic, s/he can get sick and even die.

Aviaries

Outdoor aviaries are more spacious than traditional cages and what's more important is that they allow parrots more space and offer a natural environment and fresh air.

An outdoor housing place is made up of two compartments: a net aviary (flight unit) and a shelter place. The net aviary has to be made of galvanized steel mesh and it should be 19 gauge (19G) and maximum dimension of 2.5 cm x 1.25 cm (1 x ½ in). Netting of this size should also help to keep rodents, and snakes out of the aviary, these creatures may well eat the eggs and the birds as well. To protect the aviary from predators as rats, weasels, and cats you need to bury the galvanized wire mesh deeply (at least a foot) in the ground or you will need to lay down a solid base, constructed using blocks or bricks sunk into the ground.

Ideally, the floor of the flight should be of concrete, which is much easier to clean than is grass. The aviary should have provisions for food, drinking water, bathing water, grit, perching, nesting and a place to hang a Cuttlefish bone. During the day they will perch on twigs or wooden dowels and you can offer your bird pine cones, balls, chains to play.

If you place potted plants in your aviary, the birds will spend a lot of time perching, picking and climbing, so you should provide non poisonous plants like a fruit tree, a honeysuckle bush, a privet or a forsythia. The dimensions of the flight have 3-4 metres in length (118,1 - 157,4 inches); up to 2 metres in height (78,74 inches); and between 1.2 and 1.8 metres wide (70,86 inches) width.

The perches should never be so thick that your birds cannot grip them adequately, nor so thin that the birds front toes curl right round to the back. Perches can be constructed in the shape of a `T`, and fixed in the floor, or suspended by means of wire loops attached firmly to the aviary framework. Perches should not overhang feeding utensils, because these are likely to be soiled by droppings from above. None of the wood used for perches should have been recently sprayed with chemicals. Branches are sometimes soiled by other wild birds, so it`s very important to wash them before use. In southern states of USA, outdoor caging must be protected from opossums to prevent exposure to the parasite called

Sarcocystis Falcatula, which can result in a fatal lung infection.

Roofing

The roof of the flight nearest to the shelter should be covered with translucent plastic sheeting. This will help the birds to sit outside when the weather is bad or it`s very hot. The shelter can be roofed with marine plywood, with all the cracks being filled with a waterproofing material and tarred over, before heavy-duty roofing felt is applied. This should overlap for several inches down the sides of the shelter. To ensure that the interior remains dry, guttering should be attached along the back of the sloping roof, to carry the rainwater away from the aviary.

Toys and accessories

Very inventive and always searching for something new, parrots will be happy to find in their cages all kind of toys. You have to be careful when you choose the toys, because parrots have tendency to take apart things, because every new toy is a challenge for them. When you choose toys for your parrot it's like choosing toys for a child: they have to be safe and the bird has to be happy to play with them without stressing itself. The best toys for them are pieces of softwood or perches, plastic mini balls, palm strips, twig balls, all kind of unpainted paper-made items, etc... You'll have to provide some items which helps to maintain the physical health condition of your bird:

- swings and chains which increases the capacity of movement;
- therapeutical perches which helps to maintain the bird's feet healthy;
- perches or any wood made objects which are good for chewing (if you neglect your bird by not offering him/her different objects to chew, could lead to beak deformation);
- a bowl with fresh water for bathe
- various nutritional supplements like Cuttlefish bone, seashells, etc...

One of the best game that your parrot could play is when s/he has to get out a peanut which is hidden inside of a tiny hole of a log. Your parrot has to chew the log to get inside and to get the peanut. This game makes your bird to concentrate and to work hard to eat.

You can also make your parrot happy by replacing the old toys and perches with new ones. In fact, toys and interactive games which makes your bird to work hard mentally and physically, will keep your bird healthy and svelte. Is a natural instinct for Lovebirds to destroy wood.

Chewing is a natural way for your parrot to keep its beak in good condition. So you should provide them with wood, rawhide, paper and cardboard.

They also like noisy and interactive toys like wiffle balls, music boxes, baby rattles, shape interactive toys. You can also use your imagination and create toys out of normal household items: large and clean stainless steel bolts and washers; large buttons; plastic straws; unperfumed cardboard rolls; popsicle and other wooden sticks; wrap a nut or treat into a piece of paper; plastic bottle caps with any inserts removed, etc...

You should change and rotate the toys every week to help keep your parrot interested and active. When introducing a new toy, do it slowly, because if you do it too quickly, your parrot will tend to shy away and very possibly never play with it. Their natural curiosity and wanting to see everything will encourage them to come check out the new toy with you, so make sure they see you playing with it before attaching it into the cage.

The anatomy of Lovebirds

The bird's body is covered with feathers, which helps maintain body temperature during the flight. The feathers are made out from keratin, the same protein found in our hair and nails. The feathers are covered with a thin layer of grease and feather powder. The grease is extracted with the help of the beak from the uropygial gland and distributed on the feathers. At some birds like pigeons and some species of parrots the uropygial gland is missing or is not properly developed and they have feather powder. A plumage which is permanently protected with grease or feather powder can`t become wet, because the rain will just simply flow down from it.

There are several types of feathers:

Contour feathers cover most of the surface of the bird and they protect the bird from sun, rain, wind and injury.

Flight feathers are the large feathers of the wing and tail. The tail feathers act as brakes, controlling the orientation of the flight. The flight feathers basis are covered with smaller contour feathers called coverts. There are several layers of coverts on the wings.

Down feathers are soft, fluffy and small feathers and can be found under the contour feathers.

Filoplumes are very fine, hair - like feathers.

Semiplumes provide aerodynamics, form and insulation.

Bristle feathers are usually found on the head.

The skeleton of the bird is adapted to flight function, so the bones are hollow and lightweight, without marrow inside.

In some bones, the hollow cavities contain extension of the air sacs from the lungs, which helps the bird to get the oxygen it needs to fly easily and quickly. The beak has no teeth, it`s also known as bill and it has two parts: the upper mandible and the lower mandible.

The upper mandible does not move independently from the skull while the lower mandible can move independently.

The wings of the bird are much like the arm and hand of the human.

The more important muscles are the breast muscles and those of the wings.

The breast muscles represent one third from the total body weight of the bird and they are attached to a large bone, called the keel. The keel extends from the breastbone (sternum) down along the chest and stomach.

Respiratory organs

Birds have a single nasal cavity and the larynx does not have vocal cords, it helps only to lock trachea during swallowing.

They have lungs and they have also nine air sacs through which air circulates. These air sacs allow a continuous flow of air through the respiratory system.

Digestive components

The beak serves to pick up food and for seed peeling.
The crop is the muscular pouch and it can be found at the end of the esophagus and serves as a chamber for

storing and softening food, until the food already in the stomach moves on through the rest of the digestive system.

The crop leads to a two - chambered stomach: one called proventriculus, which has the role to produce stomach enzymes for breaking food down, and the other chamber called ventriculus or gizzard, a powerful muscular organ, which takes the place of teeth and here the seeds and an assortment of grains of sand are squeezed until the seeds break up into a digestible form.

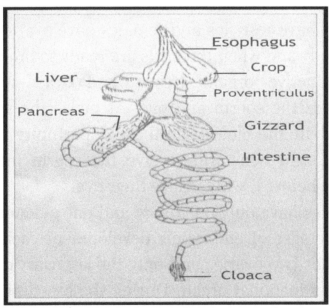

From here, the food goes through thin then thick intestine and the digested food arrives in cloaca. The cloaca is the final part of a digestive tract and it is a small chamber with a mucous membrane. Parrots excrete their feces and their urine from the cloaca and it also plays an important role in reproduction.

Urinary tract organs

The kidneys of the birds are located on both sides of the backbone and they are protected by the air sacs. The urine will be eliminated through the cloaca and it can be a soft or solid substance and it contains uric acid which makes it very corrosive.

Genital organs

Males have testicles and females have ovaries inside the body and when the birds are ready to breed, their reproductive organs (testes and ova) swell and produce the sperm and ova. At males the sperm is stored in the cloaca, until an opportunity to mate arises, and hens will receive the sperm into their cloaca before it will fertilize their ova.

Females have only one ovary and one oviduct, but in early stages of embryonic development each female bird has two ovaries and only the left ovary develops into a functional organ. During the breeding season the size of the ovary is changing, becoming larger. Males have paired abdominal testes which can be found inside of the cavity of the body. During breeding season the testes increase in size, becoming almost five times bigger than the initial size.

Body temperature is between 104 - 105.8 degrees Fahrenheit (40-41 degrees Celsius), which increase with 32.9 degrees Fahrenheit(0.5 degrees Celsius) during sexual maturity, during egg laying process and in molting period.

The eyes

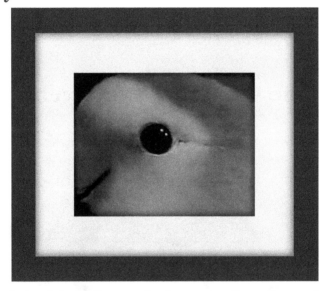

Most of the birds have their eyes placed on the side. With the help of their mobile neck bird`s can see the surroundings in a radius of 360 degrees and can fly away rapidly if there is any danger nearby.

The lower eyelid of the bird is mobile and the upper one is almost fix. The third eyelid which is called nictitating membrane is hinged at the inner side of the eye and it serves to protect the eyes from bright light, wind, etc...

The ears

The ears are tiny, round holes situated in the right and left side of the head, behind the eyes and they are covered with feathers. There are no cartilaginous pavilions, but inside the ear there is the organ of balance. When the bird suffer from ear diseases, the organ of balance is also affected. The sick bird can`t hold itself properly on the perches and its head is twisting to the affected ear.

The main diet of Lovebirds

In the wild, Lovebirds do eat primarily seeds, grass seeds, fruits, insects and other kind of vegetation. In captivity, a balanced and rational diet will insure a permanent healthy state for your bird.

The main diet of Lovebirds should consist in high quality pellets or high quality mixture of seeds (millet, oat, hemp, wheat, etc...); supplemented with fresh fruits and vegetables, daily.

There is another option for a main 100% healthy diet, like a mix of sprouted grains and seeds, raw and boiled veggies, fruits and a small amount of good quality pellets.

Place some Lovebird seeds on a container and soak the seeds in water. Spray the seeds with water to make sure they are moist. The seeds should sprout in about 5 days. Wash them before you give them to your birds.

Pellets are blend of vegetables, fruits, grains, seeds, and protein. They are baked and then formed into shapes and sizes for different species. You should always check the package for feeding instructions on pellets. The bigger your bird, the bigger the pellets should be.

Calcium deficiency is common in captive parrots, especially in birds who may have been fed only on seeds and because of the lack of the natural sunlight. Try to expose your bird to natural sunlight as much as possible and you must provide a calcium rich diet for your bird, daily. Calcium is essential for healthy bones, muscle contraction and blood clotting, nerve and heart function. You can offer them calcium - rich vegetables and fruits like broccoli, carrots, spinach, dandelion greens, mustard greens, figs, kale, endive, apricots. There are specially prepared parrot foods in the store which contain calcium.

Sometimes it can be very hard to get them to eat their veggies so you might have to spend some time encouraging your Lovebird to eat them.

It is important to provide beta-carotene vegetables on a daily basis of a Lovebird's diet, because vitamin A or beta-carotene is a common deficiency found in parrot's diet. Vegetables which are high in beta-carotene are cooked sweet potato and fresh kale. Cereals like wheat contain high level of sulphur, which can be administered to your parrot as a food supplement in molting period. The sulph helps to regenerate the plumage of the bird, that`s why you need to increase the quantity of wheat in your parrot's diet during molting period. Oat seeds contain carbohydrates and a high level of albumins, which have an important role in development of young birds. Adult parrots should have only 10% of supplementation in their diet from this cereal, because too much oat can lead to obesity. Corn seeds contain low level of vitamins and albumins, but are very rich in carbohydrates. Parrots love to eat boiled corn, you can offer them as treats. Small seeds like millet and canary seeds should be mixed with the Lovebird's regular seed mix, but be careful, too much millet seeds offered as treat could lead to obesity. Canary seeds contain carbohydrates. Fruits contain most of all sugar, which has very low quantities of nutrients.

If you don't have enough time to offer your bird a fresh diet variety every day, and you choose to feed your bird mostly with pellets, then you'll have to keep in mind that good quality pellets must represent between 60-80 % of your parrot's diet. It's better to give your bird more pellets than seeds, because pellets offer a complete nutrition. Parrots which were fed only seeds use to have a shorter lifespan, because seeds contain a high level of fat and insufficient vitamins, proteins and minerals.

Seeds have to represent no more than 12 % of your parrot's diet and they must not be dusty, or mould infested: hemp seeds, flax, sunflower, safflower, niger, canary grass, white millet, canola, etc...

Grains: rice, alfalfa, triticale, buckwheat, sesame, amaranth, quinoa.

If you decide to feed your bird with a 100% healthy diet, like sprouted seeds and grains, raw and boiled veggies, fruits and a small amount of pellets, then mix together all of the ingredients in one dish.

A half a cup of this mix is enough for a day period.

Sprouted seeds and grains provide nutrient-rich food, are lower in fat and will help balance your parrot's diet.

If the weather is too cold for sprouting, the seeds and grains can be boiled about 30 minutes instead of sprouting them.

Sprouted seeds and grains are also good in weaning period for youngsters, because the softened shell is easier to break and the young birds can get used with the texture of seeds.

Nuts and hazelnuts should be given in the same quantity as the seeds, and have to be offered in their own shell because it can be a good brain exercise for your bird: almond, cashew, pecan, pistachio, walnut. If you have a young bird, you should teach him/her how to do it, by cracking the hazelnut shell. You can offer your bird rice bread and rye bread; cereals like oats flakes or corn flakes but without sugar.

You can also make healthy homemade bird treats. For this you will need: oats, your basic bird seeds, flour, honey,water,millet.

In a plastic bowl add 2 tablespoon of oats, 2 tablespoon of bird seeds, 1 tablespoon of flour, 1 teaspoon of millets, then add half of a tablespoon of water and give it a quick mix. After that, add 1 tablespoon of honey and mix until it is fully incorporated. Add more water if it is necessary. Then roll them into small balls and put them on the baking sheet. Put them in the oven for 30 minutes at 180 degrees Celsius (356 degrees Fahrenheit).

Vegetables are very good nutrients for your bird and you can also give them frozen because they're just as nutritious as fresh veggies. During summer you can offer them fresh veggies: cucumbers, tomatoes, broccoli, carrots, green beans, pod peas, lettuce, peppers, celery, etc... Vegetables should be given in higher quantities than fruits. Lovebirds also love fresh fruits like grapes, melon, bananas, pears, nectarines, apple dices, cactus fruits, figs, pomegranate, peaches, kiwi, papayas, mango dices, strawberries, cranberries, blueberries, grapefruit, oranges, cherries, pineapple.

Bee pollen granules, banana and coconut chips are also some of the favorite foods of Lovebirds. You can also offer fresh herbs like: yarrow (Achillea millefolium), plantain (Plantago lanceolata), coltsfoot (Tussilago farfara), shepherd's purse (Capsella bursa pastoris). Leaves and branches of fruit trees, oak trees, beech trees (Fagus sylvatica), willow trees (Salix alba) are the best source of vitamins, you can provide them directly from forests. You also have to offer the opportunity to your parrot to chew these kind of branches.

During winter you can offer your bird soft food, for example, bread that was previously softened in milk and then mixed with some grated carrots, calcium and minced berries of sea-buckthorn (Hippophae rhamnoides).

Dried veggies and fruits are also good options for your bird. Lovebirds toss dried fruits and veggies into the water bowl and then eat them, once they are rehydrated. You can leave the dried veggies and fruits in the bird's cage for days, unless they get wet. Try to avoid purchasing dried veggies and fruits that contain preservatives, like sulphur dioxide.

Offer your bird once or twice per week boiled eggs. Boiled egg shells are the best source of calcium, so you can offer them to your bird in crushed form. Your parrot will love to serve some boiled chicken, beef and fish meat once or twice per week. When your bird is eating fruits, its droppings become more watery, but this should not cause alarm.

Parrots which are fed on high quality pellets usually don`t need vitamin and mineral supplementation. Over supplementation with vitamins could lead to intoxication of your bird. Supplementation with vitamins are recommended just in case when your bird`s main diet is based on seeds.

Another important thing is, never give up when you try to offer your bird new foods and it refuses them. You'll have to try more than once, by mixing the new food into other foods. Birds learn by observation and they use to watch what we eat, so they will try the new food. Human table food like scrambled eggs, and pasta are permitted if fed in small portions. Avoid giving your bird avocado, chocolate, caffeine, sugary or salty snacks, milk products and alcohol!

Uneaten food should be removed from the cages after two hours. It`s very important to have all the time in the cage some grit, because it helps with digestion.

Next, I will present 3 parrot mash recipes. You will need: 1 cup of beans, 2 cups of grains, 2-3 carrots, 1 yellow, 1 red, 1 orange pepper, 1 cauliflower, 1 broccoli, dark green leafy vegetables (dark green lettuces, cabbage, kale, italian parsley, broccoli green leaves, spinach, dandelion leaves, etc...), 2 apples, a half melon, 1 banana, 6 strawberries.

Separately soak grains and beans for about 6 hours each. Rinse each and add purified water (don't use tap water) until the beans and grains are slightly covered. Both beans and grains will soak up water, so be sure to cover them with extra water. During soaking the beans will double in size and grains swell slightly. Boil for 15 minutes uncovered, then cover and simmer for another 15 minutes. Let cool and mix beans and grains together.

Mix together the chopped vegetables and dark leafy greens with the food processor and add some water.

Then mix together the chopped apples (avoid seeds), melon, banana, strawberries.

Combine equal parts of vegetable-green mix with bean-grain mix and then add 1 cup of fruit mix for each 6 cups of the above. Mix together and then put in freezer safe containers and freeze. Thaw for 24 hours in refrigerator before use. Do not use a microwave to thaw.

For the second recipe of parrot mash you will need:

½ cooked sweet potato, 4-5 teaspoon of fully cooked grains (oats, quinoa seeds, brown rice, wheat, rye), 2 teaspoon of chopped veggies (cauliflower, broccoli, red, orange, yellow peppers, carrot, zucchini, etc...), 1 teaspoon of unsweetened apple sauce.

With a fork, mash ½ cooked sweet potato and mix together with 4-5 teaspoon of fully cooked grains. If it is too dry, then you can add a little water. You can also add 1 teaspoon of unsweetened apple sauce and mix.

The third one is " Sweet potato balls" and for this recipe you will need:

1 cooked sweet potato, 1 mashed banana, ½ cup raisins, 1 cup mixed fresh or frozen vegetables (celery; carrots; red, yellow, orange peppers; zucchini; broccoli; cauliflower; green peas; etc...), 1 cup diced apples, 1 and ½ cup uncooked oatmeal and corn flakes.

Mix all together and add some fruit juice to make it form small balls. You'll have to freeze balls individually. Defrost them before serving.

Cleaning your parrot's house

Your beloved parrot could be easily affected by the bacterias which can live in the cage during the day, that`s why you need to clean it every day and a more complex clean every week. The floor of the cage, the food and water recipients should be cleaned daily.

I recommend that the floor of the cage should be covered with kitchen paper towel, or paper sheets which can be changed daily. The disinfection of the cage, and food and water recipients must be made with hot water weekly.

Don't use disinfection products very often because they are toxic for your parrot! When you do so, be careful and move the bird in a different room. It`s very important to use eye protection glasses and gloves when the disinfection operation is taking place, because it can cause serious injuries.

You can use bleach for disinfection, but be aware to not mix it with other chemical products, because it`s very dangerous. You can use the bleach in diluted form: 30 ml of bleach mixed with 250ml of water. This mixture will be very efficient to combat bacterias and viruses. After you finish with the disinfection process, it`s very important to rinse well with cold water the recipients and the cage.

Breeding

Lovebirds reach sexual maturity at 1 year old. They are usually reproducing all year long, but most of them are likely to do so in winter time or the beginning of spring. Breeding season takes place during the months of March and April. They will breed in shadowy places or in nesting boxes. The peached-face female use to tucks the nesting materials into its rump feathers.

Hens usually lay between 2-6 eggs, the egg sitting period last for 22 days. The hen feeds the babies from hatching to the age of 3-4 weeks. The hatchlings are blind and naked. The pair will need to be provided with plenty of food, especially soft food to allow them to feed their youngsters.

Lovebirds always feed their babies while sitting on their backs. The youngsters need to be hand fed until they are 8 weeks old. From this age you can begin to wean them onto soft pellets, millet, fresh veggies and fruits.

Lovebirds require nesting boxes with dimensions of 7.87 x 7.87 x 9.84 inches (20 x 20 x 25 cm) and the entrance hole should be 6 cm in diameter.

The size of the cage has to be at least 23.6 x 23.6x 35.4 inches (60 x 60 x 90 cm). The nest box should have a removable top lid for nest inspection. Nesting materials such as pine or wood shavings, dried plant materials, should cover the bottom of the nest box. Double entrance boxes are often used to reduce the chance of the male trapping the female in the nesting box. During breeding season, males become aggressive, so clipping their wings will help the females to escape.

How to hand feed a baby parrot

The maximum quantity which has to be given to a baby parrot before the weaning period has to be 10% of its body weight. The crop of the most baby parrots usually gets empty between 4-6 hours. You'll have to stop feeding the bird during night time, between midnight and 6 o'clock, (pause of 6 hours), period which will allow the crop to empty of residual food. In this time you'll have enough time to get rest. As the baby parrot grows, you'll have to reduce the number of feeding times, but you'll have to increase a little bit more the quantity of food.

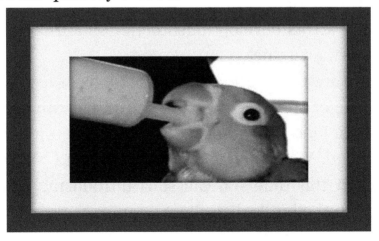

The most important thing is to control the quantity of food offered at each meal. Don`t offer more food than 10% of the bird's body weight in a meal. As the baby parrot grows, it will refuse to be hand feed and you'll have to stop with hand feeding or you'll have to reduce them. When you are at the stage of only 2-3 hand feedings, offer your bird solid food (softened pellets) or cooked food. In 2-3 weeks time, your bird should be able to get used with solid food and you can completely skip the evening meals.

How to prepare the hand feeding formula:

Use commercially prepared hand feeding formula which is specifically created for Lovebird babies.

You should use a thermometer to ensure that the hand feeding formula is warm enough (about 102 to 105 degrees Fahrenheit).

Use the microwave to heat up the water, add measured amount of formula and stir. Make sure you feed at the right temperature.

Baby parrots develop much better on a thin formula rather than a thick one.

There are two most common methods of feeding: by syringe or spoon. Allowed the bird to breath between bites of food and stop feeding when the crop is nicely rounded. You can feed this formula up to 7 weeks of age. At this time you can start introducing weaning food in the bird's diet. Start weaning your baby with veggies, seeds, fruits and good quality pellets. Grains and sprouted seeds are also a good start in weaning your baby parrot, because the softened shell is easier to break. Place a separate water dish next to his food. Any remains must be removed after 3 hours. At 9-10 weeks of age your baby parrot should be placed on a single feeding per day. At this time pellets and seed mix should be its favorite food. Serve fruits and veggies cut in small pieces.

You can serve warm moistened pellets early in the morning at 8am and 4pm.

At the age of 12 weeks old your bird should be eating on its own.

During weaning period some babies can lose up to 15% of their weight.

It is important to keep an eye on your young bird regularly, regarding feeding. Watch your young bird weight, until it is 5 months old. Take your bird in your hand at least once a day and feel its breast bone by moving your hand from side to side across his/her chest. A healthy young parrot should have its breast bone covered with soft muscles on each side of it.

When you want to bring home a young Lovebird, make sure the feed pots are placed on the bottom of the cage. The climbing skill are not yet developed and so the easiest way to feed themselves will be from the pots placed on the bottom of the cage. Set up the cage with the perches placed down low, until your bird learns to climb around.

Other foods can also be offered to your baby, like chopped hard boiled egg, scrambled egg, chopped roast chicken breast, white boneless fish, boiled rice or pasta, biscuit crumbs, millet spray, boiled sweet potato mash.

Here is a delicious recipe for young Lovebirds:

1 and 1/2 cups fresh corn

1 cup brown rice

1/2 cup dried mango or banana

2 and 1/2 tbsp raisins

3 and 1/2 tbsp split lentils or peas

2 and 1/2 tbsp unsalted pistachio nuts

1 tsp dried powdered milk

Bring 0.5 liters of water to boil, add all contents, cover and boil gently for 30 minutes. Serve warm or cool.

MOLTING

The molting process can take place once or twice per year, which usually don`t have any effect on the birds flying capacity.

The natural molting happens when the warm season ends and the colder season starts to appear. In this period of the year birds will change all their feathers. The molting will take place gradually, at some birds it will take from 2 to 3 months (March - June) and it could happen after the birds have hatched their eggs and after rearing their youngsters. This process is influenced by the hormones of thyroid gland and the genital organs. In this period they`ll need proper diet like camomile tea (Matricaria Chamomilla), St John's wort tea (Hypericum Perforatum), amino acid like methionine, hemp seeds and vitamins like A, D, E.

They also become very stressed when molting takes place, and makes them vulnerable to new diseases. In this period they are cleaning themselves persistently and have a more quiet behavior. When normal molting is taking place, there should never be bald patches present on the bird's body. The new feathers that are replacing the old feathers, are called blood feathers. If the blood feather is cut or injured it can bleed in excess. If your bird has broken blood feathers, you'll have to ask for your avian vet help.

All he has to do is to pull the broken feather out and apply some pressure with a gauze square to stop the bleeding. When your parrot is molting it could have many pin feathers present especially on the back of its head because a single parrot can`t preen the normally present feather sheaths from the back of the head. You can help your parrot by removing gently the feather sheaths with your index finger and thumb. You have to be very careful when you are doing this operation, because it could be very painful for your bird.

How to maintain your parrot's health

The first sign of disease

There are several physical and behavioral signs about the bird's illness:

-depressed attitude and unusual irritability;

-they sleep more than 10-12 hours per day, with their head hidden under the wing

- they keep their eyes almost shut all the time and the wings hang from the body

- don`t have the same stability on their legs and they spend more time as usual on the bottom of the cage
- their appetite is reduced and they are losing weight
- don't clean their plumage and their feet
- excessive cough and sneeze and nose secretion dripping
- the feathers around the beak and the vent are dirty
- eye discharge, swollen eyes
- their feces colour differs from normal and they present diarrhoea
- excessive moulting
- discoloration of the feathers
- breathing difficulties

When you recognize these signs, you should contact your vet doctor for a precise diagnosis.

Few advices about how to keep your parrots healthy

The most important condition to keep your birds healthy is a proper diet. Choosing the appropriate cage and the right environment are very important factors. A smaller cage than usual can cause agitation and the bird will try to escape.

The cage must be kept clean, to avoid bacterial infestation. Daily flying exercises is needed.

Watch out, your ornamental plants: philodendron, iris and yellow daffodil could be poisonous for your birds. Cigarette smoke, hair spray (hair lacquer), body spray, furniture spray, vapors of household cleaners like bleach, should be avoided, when the birds are around. Avoid exposing your cage with your parrot outside when there are dangerous cats around because they can easily knock down the cage.

Learn about the natural habits of your bird, for example you can find out if your bird love to have bath most often than showers, then you have to place a bowl filled with water in the cage, or for the other option you'll have to spray him/her with water very often. Try to discover and offer your bird the most favorite and natural foods as possible and make available natural environments for it.

Make regular veterinary examinations, because birds can hide the signs of diseases. In the wild sick birds used to hide any sign of their disease, they even try to eat with the rest of the flocks, because there is a risk to lose their life (the others will steal his food and bite him because they feel his weakness). The cage birds can act the same way, they look like they are healthy, they eat very well, until one day they could fall off from the perches. Even when they have sharp pains, they don't tend to exteriorize their feelings. The bird plumage can hide the eventually weight losses caused by diseases.

If you recognize the signs presented above, you better visit your avian vet as soon as possible. Sometimes a routine examination can help to discover any latent infection of the bird.

How to recognize the abnormal droppings

Feces and urine are eliminated by your bird at the same time. The color of feces depend of the assimilation of the food and it can vary from dark green and brown, to black. On the feces usually there is a white urine patch. If the darker part of the feces is more liquid, then the bird has diarrhoea. When the urine appears like a lake around the fecal material, there could be kidney problems. There could be situations when you have to visit your avian vet for routine examinations (check-ups) and because of the stress, the droppings of your bird could have a very liquid form, but just for a short period of time and it will normally pass away. In this case we don't talk about diseases. For a precise examination you better visit your avian vet.

Feather picking and self -mutilation

When a bird moves its beak through the feathers making them clean, then we talk about preening. But when the bird starts to pay too much attention to its feathers by pulling them out obsessively, then we talk about self-mutilation.

There could be several causes to this problems like: skin diseases, stress or internal diseases. When the main cause is the skin itchiness, among the special treatments prescribed by your avian vet, you can also apply directly on the bird's skin some anesthetic powder. In this period you'll have to avoid placing the cage near radiators or in direct sunlight, because the bird's skin will become excessively dry.

How to catch and manipulate your parrot without hurting it

There are many situations when you'll have to catch and hold the bird in your hands. First of all, you have to remove all the accessories from the cage, including: the water and feeding bowls, the mirror and other things. The easiest method to catch the bird without stressing it is to create darkness and turn the power off in the room where the bird is located. Before you turn the power off, you'll have to know exactly where the bird is located. You can catch him/her very easy because s/he can`t see very well in the dark. You can also use a scarf by placing it on the head of your parrot to be able to grab carefully the neck then to fix the head. With the other hand you'll have to hold the legs with which s/he can cause serious injuries. For this procedure you'll have to use some leather made gloves. It is generally better to grab them by the neck than by the belly because parrot's neck is extremely strong, flexible and mobile, and it has more vertebrae, than humans or mammals. The neck is considered to be the strongest part of a parrot`s body. Birds breathe by expanding the rib cage outward, which draws air in. That`s why is so important when you examine or try to clip your bird's wings to avoid pressing the chest area, because it will not be able to breathe. They have a very strong beak and neck so they can hang on your fingers without any problem. When you are carrying them around restrained you can hold them on their back, this is also useful for when you need to groom your parrot, or check its wings. For the examination of the bird there`s need for two persons: one to hold the bird and one for the examination: Check both wings of the bird, first by open the left and then the right wing like a fan and check the feathers. With a magnifying glass you can check for ticks. You can also check the breast muscle by touching it very gently. In the middle part of the chest there is the sternum. If you feel that the stern is very sharp, then we can talk about malnutrition (the bird is sick from a longer period of time or doesn't receive enough food).

You can also check for the cloacal opening the common orifice through which is eliminate the feces and urine, and at females the eggs passes just through the same opening. The feathers from this area must be clean, if they are not, it means that the bird suffer from diarrhea. You'll have to check the belly, which is under the stern, by pressing it very gently. It normally has to be soft and flat, if it's bumped over the stern level and it's firm, then there could be a sign of a tumor.

Eczemas or injuries can be found easily if you blow some air under the feathers and you can check for any injuries or lumps on the bird's skin. You can check for abscesses on the foot, which can be uncomfortable for your bird.

How to choose the right avian vet

The best way to choose the right avian vet is by asking your friends, which already own birds for a longer period of time.

When you call the vet, ask him if he is a bird expert.

What should you know, when you inform your vet

Before visiting your vet, you have to be prepared with some information about your bird. You have to know your bird`s age, if not, an experienced vet will help you with this.

The vet will ask you a few questions like:

- Since how long do you own the bird?
- Where are they from?
- Do you have any other pets?
- You bought recently another bird?
- There was health problems in your family?
- Since when appeared the symptoms and what are the main signs of disease?
- The bird was treated before by you or by other vet?
- What kind of food you give to the bird?
- Did the bird participate in an exhibition show?

- There`s a member of your family sick ? (fever, diarrhea)

It`s very important to visit the same vet every time your bird presents health problems, because this way he can follow the bird's evolution.

Microchipping your parrot

Microchip is a very small electronic device encased in a glass chamber, about the size of a rice grain, which is inserted into a bird. When a scanner is passed over the area of the body containing the chip, it is activated and it transmits an identification number and the name of the chip manufacturer to the scanner's display screen. The person scanning then using the manufacturer database will locate the contact informations of the owner. Make sure the scanned microchip number matches with the number on the computerized paper strip that goes in the brochure which the client takes home. You can also ask your avian vet to check periodically the proper functionality of the microchip. The microchip is implanted (on the left side) into the pectoral muscle of the bird or under the wings. The procedure is much like an injection and it last about 10 seconds; the chip is implanted through a hypodermic needle. It can be done without the use of anesthetics, but many vets prefer to anesthetize to ensure proper placement. If you are changing your address and phone number, don't forget to announce your vet or specialist from the animal shelter to register your new address. Microchips are not GPS devices, they're for the purpose of identifying founded birds. Birds which are founded and taken to the animal shelters are scanned for microchips before they're adopted. It is recommended that you use a widely known brand increasing the probability that a scanner for that brand is available.

How to take care of the beak and the nails of your parrot

The bird's beak and nails grow continuously, so you have to take care of them, throughout your bird's life. To prevent the beak to grow excessively you need to place a cuttlefish bone in the cage, which is also good as high calcium intake or you can cut it back carefully with a strong pair of scissors. When trimming process is taking place, for a safer results (to avoid injuries) there`s need for two persons to hold the bird.

Parrots have a predisposition for excessive beak growth, you'll have to cut it very often almost every four weeks. Because of the long beak parrots can`t eat properly and they could die because of that.

Before trimming the beak, dab it with slightly warm glycerin or olive oil. When nails overgrow, you need to cut them very carefully with a special scissor without causing any injuries. Overgrowth nails lead to instability on the perches or even the impossibility to walk. When trimming the nails it's best to cut off a little at a time.

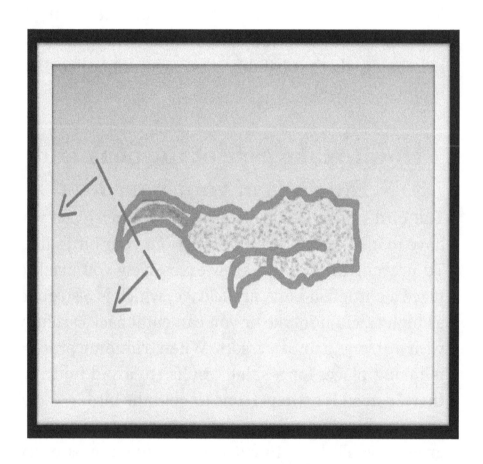

You have to know that the birds nails contains (at the base of it) very fine blood vessels and nerves, which makes them very sensitive.

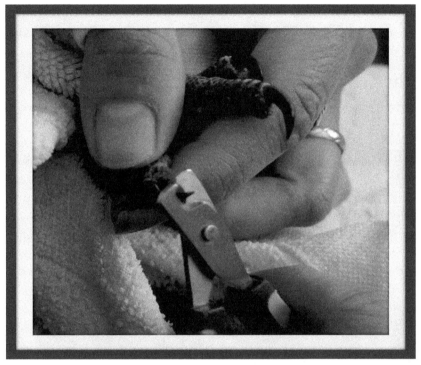

If by mistake, you cut too much from the bird's nails, they will bleed and the bird will feel the same pain as we do when we over cut our nails. In this case you can stop the bleeding by using cotton buds soaked in vitamin K or C.

For a better result, when you cut the nails, you can grease your bird's toes with comestible oil, to soften them.

How to clip your parrot's wings

If your parrot mostly lives in an aviary and you don't interact with it, then clipping the wing is unnecessary. The main purpose of wing clipping is to prevent fast and upward flight.

Wing clipping is safe if it is performed properly. If you don`t know how to clip your bird's wing, the best way is to find an avian vet, who is experienced in the art of wing clipping. If you decide to do it by yourself then you'll have to study about the bird's wing shape and about terminology of its feathers.

You'll also need a competent assistant who will help holding the bird. Avoid clipping the primary and secondary coverts, and secondary feathers on both wings. With the help of your assistant wrap the bird in a towel and hold it by the neck.

Be careful the bird's chest must not be restricted because it can`t breathe and carefully liberate one wing which has to be held at the base of the humerus and not by the feathers.

If you don`t hold the wing correctly, you can cause serious injuries, if the bird try to flap its wing.

You can leave intact the last three primary feathers (P10,P9,P8) and clip the next four primary feathers (P7,P6,P5,P4) or you can clip the first four primary feathers (P7,P8,P9,P10) and you can leave the other primary feathers intact. Do the same process on the other wing.

Bathing your parrot

In the wild parrots can take a bathe in rainy days by opening their wings and tail sideways or they can have a bathe in little natural ponds on uneven ground.

In captivity, you have to provide different ways to keep your bird clean. You can spray them or you can give them a shower, but you should be careful because the upper respiratory tract and the sinuses are quite exposed. You can provide them artificial ponds by using not too deep water bowls or you can also use the sink or the bathtub. However your bird will still love to have a bathe in its drinking water bowl.

Lovebirds will let you know which way they prefer and enjoy their bath time.

Always, make sure that you use room-temperature water, do not use warm or hot water, because it will dry out their skin so they itch and can cause feather plucking / picking. The importance of giving a shower is to get them clean and encourage them to preen their feathers.

In outside aviaries some parrots enjoy a sprinkler system overhead or getting lightly sprayed with a water hose.

During bath and shower time parrots will typically fluff up their feathers to allow the water to penetrate through the feathers and to their skin. After bath time, your parrot will start preening and getting its feathers back in the position they normally were.

It is recommended that your bird to be bathed during daytime and given time to dry completely. Some parrots would most likely prefer to get showered on a daily basis. For other birds, a good bath or shower once or twice a week will be enough.

During molting periods, your bird will become very itchy due to the new feathers coming out. You should increase bath time during this period, as it will help keep the itchiness down and also make the feather sheaths soft, making it easier for your parrot to remove them. Let your bird dry off naturally or with the help of a towel and make sure that your bird is placed in a warm room of the house. Then let your bird have the chance to preen and get its feathers back in place.

The use of blow dryer can lower their skin moistness and there is also the danger of possibly burning their skin.

Some parrots are scared to get wet, so if your bird doesn't like to bathe, then wait until it rains and lightly mist them with the spray bottle. Because they like to imitate us, just go ahead and get yourself wet or let them see you splash in the water. It is very important to not force your bird to bathe.

Sometimes your parrot will get dirty and greasy, in these kind of situations you'll have to use special shampoos. The best shampoos are those for children. There are also several special products for your bird, but be careful of those which contains oils and perfumes, because your bird could perceive them as detrimental substances and it may start to pull out his/her own feathers. You'll have to dilute a little bit of shampoo in the bathing water and easily sprinkle your bird with it until it became all wet. Leave the bird about five minutes in a warm place, then rinse it well with clean warm water. If your bird is excessively dirty (oil, ink, liquid glue, etc..) then you'll have to visit your avian vet as soon as possible.

The special needs of the parrots

Flying exercises

Parrots belong to flying birds category, so they'll need to fly very often. So if you have a small cage in your house, you'll have to assure them with almost daily flying exercises, to maintain their well being.

A room with well closed windows will surely be enough for them. You have to avoid to agglomerate a small cage with lots of birds and toys. If you can't afford a bigger cage then one pair of parrots should be enough for you. As long as they're two they will be alright.

Free flight will prevent muscle atrophy of the wings and chest, and it will maintain the bird in a good physical condition.

When you leave your bird outside of the cage, serious precautions have to be taken, because your bird could be everywhere, for example on the couch where it can be crashed, when he is hiding between the pillows.

Another important problem, is the kitchen for them, you should not leave the birds in the kitchen, especially when you are cooking, because they can fall into a hot pan from the cooker. They love to sit on top of the doors, so you have to be careful when you close the door of your room.

Before the first flight you have to place your bird close to the window to get used with it, otherwise it will try to fly through the window and serious accidents could happen. You can also cover the window with some curtains to avoid accidents. In the wild, parrots use to "work" to provide their food, to build their nest, to fly and care for young ones. You'll have to make sure that your parrot will perform some exercises for five minutes, a few times every day.

Wing flapping: try to lower your hand up and down to encourage flapping. You can swing your parrot around in a circle or back and forth by making your bird to flap its wings a few times a day. You can also place a blanket on the floor and chase your parrot around. They'll love this game.

You can also encourage your bird to dance with you and with your children. Your parrot will be very happy to dance and jump around and also will become tired. Make sure that children and parrots are supervised.

Bedding materials

In the wild the birds have less contact with their droppings, because they have unlimited space. In captivity, their droppings could affect the bird's health by distribution of microbes and parasites.

The loose sand or absorbent paper are the best bedding materials, you should avoid using newspaper, because it contains lead (chemical substance), which could be dangerous for your bird.

Parrots will need daily portion of grit in their cage, to help with digestion, which will have to be changed daily because there will be droppings on them, and this way you can maintain your birds healthy life.

The everyday life of parrots

During the day Lovebirds will play by climbing on perches, sing or will wait for the owners to return home.

In the wild parrots get up at sunrise and go to sleep at sunset.

In captivity you have to respect the day and night program of the bird. So you have to be sure that your bird will spend most of the day in a room exposed to light and for that you can place the cage close to the window.

At nighttime they will need a room without any illumination and noise source, to have a good sleep.

If you stay up for long and you have to use the light in the same room where the birds are, you better cover the cage with a thin piece of curtain material to help them sleep. You can use that piece of material also in daytime, to cover the half part of the cage, which will help the bird to take shelter from the direct sunlight when the weather is hot.

Inappropriate perches

In the wild the birds sit on different sizes of branches, which are very comfortable for them. In captivity they spend almost all the time on the perch, which could be too slippery, too thick or too thin for the bird's feet. All this imperfections can cause swelling of the feet and deformities of the joints.

To avoid these problems, you can place big branches in the cage, but first you'll have to peel their bark and for disinfection you'll have to pour hot water on them. It's good to have different sized perches in the cage because it will stimulate the blood circulation and it will exercise the parrot's feet. Sandy perches may dry out the feet and make them sore if they are the only perches provided in your parrot's cage. These perches have fantastic value if they are positioned in the right place.

What you can do if your parrot is escaping from the cage

How to prevent the escape

First of all you have to clip your parrot's wings to avoid high altitude flights and to assure an easy landing on the floor. You must always make sure that all the windows are well shut. Don't let out a bird if its wings are not clipped. When somebody is knocking at your door, before you open it, place the bird back in the cage. They could be scared sometimes when they see strangers and they can fly outside through the door.

Make sure that your parrot can`t get out of the cage, some birds are extremely intelligent and they're able to open the cage door with their beak, so you'll have to provide some locker for the cage door.

When your friends are visiting you at home, you better lock the cage for the bird`s sake, to avoid escaping through the open windows. In case that your bird could escape, you have to have some recent pictures taken with your parrot.

What you can do if your parrot has already escaped

If your bird just simply disappeared, then take the cage outside and put some fresh food and water in it, maybe your bird will try to return.

If your bird is on the nearest tree, then you can sprinkle some water on it with garden hose. Be careful, the overpressure of the water can cause serious injuries to your bird!

Be sure that you have all the necessary equipment at hand in case that the bird is reappearing: towels, cage, nest, etc...

Contact your closest neighbours to give them detailed description about your missing parrot and make sure that everybody knows your address and phone number to contact you in case that they found your bird.

Make posters with the bird detailed description and place them on light posts as far as possible around your area on main and side roads, shop stores, churches. Your children can help you by offering posters to their colleagues at school.

Ring local vets and give them your phone number and pet details.

Walk around your local area calling your bird, don't forget that your bird is very scared and you'll have to call her very often, because even if s/he will hear you, s/he will not answer back to you for the first time. You'll have to return in the same places to call your bird again and again. Drop your poster into letterboxes in your area.

If you manage to find your bird, you'll have to visit your avian vet as soon as possible for a detailed examination and for wing clipping.

How to administer medication to your parrot

There are a few possible methods about how to administer medication to your parrot:

Adding medication in drinking water

Adding medication in drinking water is a controversial method, but sometimes this is the only available method. The purpose is for the bird to take the medicine during the day directly from the drinking water. There are lots of disadvantages of this method. The bitter taste of the water makes the bird to refuse to drink it. Some birds will refuse to drink water, if its color has changed. Another disadvantage is that the water-medicine mixture has to be prepared and changed daily. There is a risk that your bird could dehydrate.

Adding medication in food

This method is better than the one with water, because you can hide the medicine in the favorite food of your parrot. Usually you can mix suspensions (liquid medicines), tablets or the content of a capsule in food.

The disadvantage of this method is that the bird could refuse to eat the food mixed with medicine, because it changed the food taste. It could be difficult to mix the medicine with the food, because of the hard consistency of the medicine, and could be needed to add some water to soften the medicine.

The other disadvantage is, if there are several birds in the cage, all the others may eat from the medicine-food mixture. If a healthy bird is more authoritative, it could eat most of the food-medicine mixture, while the sick bird will receive too little.

Liquid medication (Suspensions)

This is the best method to administer liquid medication to your bird directly through the beak. The most oral suspensions are accepted very well by the birds, especially those with good taste.

You'll have to follow the next procedure:

Fill the syringe or pipette with the prescribed quantity of suspension. There should be no needle on the syringe. Before you try restraining your bird, it`s worth seeing if s/he will accept the suspension from the syringe through the cage bars. If not, you'll have to take out your parrot from its cage and wrap it in a towel, only the head and the chest of the bird will be uncovered and the chest also needs to be able to rise and fall in order for your bird to breathe. Before you start to administer the suspension, you'll have to wait until the bird calms down. You'll have to place the syringe at the left or right side of the beak, (it`s possible that bird will bite it at first) and after you managed to place it in the interior of the beak, you can administer the suspension very slowly. You'll have to allow the bird to swallow frequently, because if you squeeze the suspension too fast, the medicine can get into the lungs and the bird could die.

It`s possible to observe that the suspension is getting out through the nostrils of the bird. Don't panic, just stop giving any medicine to your bird and leave it to calm down. Try to call your avian vet and tell him about what happened. If you can't reach your avian vet, then don't administer any medicine to your bird at that moment, until you speak with a specialized avian vet.

Injectable medications

Another method to administering medication is through repeated injections. Usually this kind of method is not used very often, (only in emergency cases) because the bird is exposed at repeated stress because of the pain.

Vitamins and minerals excess or deficiency

The insufficient or too much quantity of vitamin intake can cause serious health problems to the birds. The owners have to assure them an optimal intake of vitamins and minerals.

Vitamin A

Vitamin A deficiency is considered the main cause of diseases at cage birds. In the bird's body, the carotene is transformed in vitamin A.

Sources: provitamin A: fish fat or cod liver oil; egg

yolk, carrots, green plants, vegetables, sunflower seeds;

Diseases: avitaminosis A: drying of the surface of the eyeball, eyelid edema, infections of the mucous membranes, rhinitis, sinusitis, white membranes inside the beak, kidney problems and gout (gout occurs in birds when uric acid level becomes too high in their blood stream), swollen feet, diarrhoea, fluffed plumage; in molting period the slow growth process of feathers.

Properties: protects the mucous membranes, the eyes and skin;

Administration: fish fat or cod liver oil 3-4 drops through the beak;

Vitamin B complex:

Sources: cereal germs, rice bran, raw egg yolk, carrots, oranges, other fruits, fresh cottage cheese, cooked liver, beer yeast.

The beer yeast must be dissolved in warm water before the administration. The preventive doses must be administered daily, until the bird will be perfectly healthy: 5-10 years old bird must have 50 mg beer yeast/day; 11-20 years old bird must have 100-150 mg beer yeast /day; 21-30 years old bird must have 200-250 mg beer yeast/day; 31-40 years old bird must have 300-350 mg beer yeast/day; 41-50 years old bird must have 400-450 mg beer yeast/day; 51-60 years old bird must have 500-550 mg beer yeast/day; 60-70 years old bird must have 550-600 mg beer yeast/day; 70 years old bird must have 650-800 mg beer yeast/day.

Diseases: the bird can`t keep its head straight;

 -avitaminosis B1: slowing growth rate, body weight loss, nerve problems, paralysis, spasms, digestive disorders, diarrhoea;

Properties: it`s given during hatching period, in growth period, in prolonged treatments with antibiotics, to protect the intestinal flora;

- B5- in circulatory disorders;
- B12- in period of growth, agitation and depression;

Administration of B5 and B12 is given in liquid form, a couple of drops through the beak or in drinking water. You must add 1-2 ml of B complex in 50-100 ml of water for 3-5 days.

Vitamin C

Sources: green plants, bananas, grapes, blackcurrant, rose hips, parsley;

Diseases: the fragility of very small blood vessels, hematomas, tiredness;

Properties: increases immunity, strengthens the capillary wall;

Administration: feeding with green plants

Vitamin D

Sources: green plants, egg yolk, fish flour, beer yeast; exposure of the bird of natural sunlight;

Diseases: slowing growth, fluffed plumage, rachitis, bone fragility, calcium deposits, lack or softening of the egg shell;

Administration: fish fat or cod liver oil - first a few drops through the beak, then mixed with food ;

Vitamin K

Sources: hemp seeds, dill, fruits, spinach,

Diseases: slow clotting - prolonged bleedings in subcutaneous tissue;

Properties: it`s important in blood clotting;

Vitamin E

Sources: maize, cereal germs, yolk, butter, vegetables;

Diseases: decrease of fecundity - atrophy of embryo in egg; loss of coordination of muscles, walking in circles.

First aid kit for your parrot

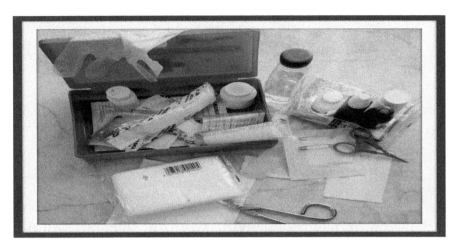

It`s very important to have a first aid kit in your house, because sadly accidents could happen sometimes. First, you'll have to call your avian vet, but you have to be ready to use your first aid kit in case that your bird require immediate medical care in cases like burn or injury of one of the wings.

The first aid kit has to contain the following items:

- electric birds pillow, to warm up the bird to treat shocks; in case that your bird is very sick don't leave it unattended on the pillow, because there is a danger of   overheating.

-Pedialyte (electrolyte solution for children), these kind of solution has to be given at room temperature

- eye drops (medication) and eye wash (to clean the eyes)

- eyedropper
- cotton swabs and balls to clean the open wound
- scissors

-gauze rolls to bandage scratches, burns or open wounds

-tweezers to remove broken blood feathers

-antiseptic wipes

-betadine or iodine solution

-medical tape

-masking tape

- 3% hydrogen peroxide solution to clean wounds. When you clean the wound for the first time, you'll have to use the undiluted form of the solution. After that you'll have to
dilute the hydrogen peroxide solution with water 1:10.

-medical first aid pen flashlight, to see inside of the bird's mouth

-antibiotic ointment to prevent infection of cuts and scratches

-syringe (without needle on top), feeding tubes, pipettes. You have to be well prepared before you use feeding tubes.

-towels

-hand feeding formula (mature birds can get 5% of their body weight at one feeding, once or twice per day.

-latex gloves

-animal poison control center phone number

-magnifying glass

-heating lamp

-bird`s medical records

-parrot`s first aid book

Trauma at parrots

The main cause of the diseases suffered by birds is the accidents. The birds left unattended can hit the windows or cut themselves in different kind of objects.

When the bird suffered a trauma without bleeding, then it has to calm down and stay warm.

When the bird is bleeding, for example, when breaking a leg or wing, first you have to stop the bleeding, then you have to calm the bird down. When the bird suffered a cranial trauma, you don't have to place it in a warm place, because he will need a dark and quiet place.

To stop the bleeding you'll need to apply a cotton cloth on the wound, by pressing it for 5 - 10 minutes. The cotton cloth soaked in vitamin K, is more efficient. Cuts and scratches must be cleaned with iodine. If your bird is covered with a grease substance, then you have to wash and dry it or you can apply some talcum powder on it.

In all the above situations try to find a vet as soon as possible.

Poor general condition

The normal body temperature of the birds is 105.8 degrees Fahrenheit (41 degrees Celsius).

When they get sick, the body temperature drops too much, that's why you need to measure your bird's body temperature, when you observe this kind of problems. All you have to do, is to increase the bird's body temperature, when it`s too low. You'll have to cover one part of the cage with a thick towel, then you'll have to place a desk lamp with a 75 - 100 W bulb at 10 cm close to the bird. The room has to be heated, the temperature could be between 77-95 degrees Fahrenheit (25 - 35 degrees Celsius).

Forced feeding

When the birds are sick they usually refuse to eat, this could be a big problem because they can't survive for long without food.

It is therefore necessary to force your bird to eat, with viscous consistency mashed food, which is given little by little, with a syringe without needle on top. You can feed your parrot for 3-4 times per day with approximately 5-10 ml of liquid food. If you don`t know how to feed your bird you better ask your avian vet to show you how to forced feed your bird. Because forced feeding is very stressing for birds, it has to be done just in case that the bird hasn't eat for 2-3 days.

Parasites

External parasites

External parasites or ectoparasites can be divided into lice, mites and the rest. Lice infestations appears as small, brownish colored insects that can be seen moving through your bird's feathers. Sometimes you can't see lice with your naked eyes, you just simply notice excessive itching in your bird. Bird lice lay their eggs at the base of the feather and the egg developing period could take for up to 6 weeks.

The most common mite seen on birds is Cnemidocoptes- the Scaly Face / Leg mite, which feeds on keratin, the protein that makes up the surface layer of the skin, beak and feet. Left untreated the Scaly Face mite can cause disruption of the growth areas of the beak, leading to distortion of the beak. Thickening of the scales on the legs can lead to pain.

In massive infestation appears the total or partial loss of feathering.

The combat of parasites can be done with treatments with Ivermectin or Moxidectin, which can be applied on the skin on the back of the neck or put in the bird's drinking water.

This type of parasites don't have any affects on humans.

Syringophilus bipectinatus which feed on feather and skin excess and they can be located between live feathers brushes and tail feathers. May occur malformation of feathers, which could be treated with Ivermectin.

Dermanyssus gallinae, the red bird mite appears mostly at aviary birds, which do not live on the bird's body. During the day, they are hiding in cracks and crevices around aviaries. Massive infestation takes place during summer. The treatment must be done with insecticides in aviary, before the birds were previously moved, after disinfection you need to rinse the aviary with water. The birds will be treated with powder which contains Pyrethrum. Decontamination will be repeated after 7 days. To prevent parasitic reinfestation after you finished the prescribed treatment with your bird, you'll have to thoroughly clean the bird's cage by disinfecting all its surfaces, corners and bars of the cage.

Internal parasites

Gapeworm (Syngamus Trachea)

It`s a disease caused by a worm called Syngamus trachea, which is located in the trachea of the affected bird. The gapeworm also affects turkeys, geese, cage birds, wild birds, especially wild pheasants. Infestation occurs when there are wild pheasants close to your birds or indirectly by intermediate hosts like earthworms and snails.

Gapeworms are located in the trachea, bronchi and the lungs. Gurgling noises that come from the throat of the bird are caused by the gapeworm infestation, and it can be confused with respiratory problems.

Symptoms: difficult breathing with open beak, cough, anemia, anorexia, weakness; if there is a heavy infestation with gapeworms, then the bird could die by suffocation.

Treatments: Thiabendazole powder in feed. Fenbendazole (Panacur) for 3 days. Flubendazole for youngsters in feed for 7 days. Febantel (Rintal) in feed for 7 days. Tetramisole-Nilverm administered in water for 3 days. Disinfection and dry maintenance of the aviary or cage is required.

Trichomoniasis (Trichomonas gallinae):

This parasite is located in the sinuses, mouth, throat, crop, intestine and liver of the bird. Among domestic birds, there are also wild birds which are infested with this kind of internal parasite (sparrows, vultures, seagulls, wild doves, etc...).

Symptoms: white or yellow cheesy-looking nodules inside of the mouth and throat; reduced appetite; excessive mucus in the mouth, esophagus and crop; vomiting; dehydration; weight loss; diarrhoea; respiratory disorders; even death. Treatments: you must gently remove the cheesy deposits from the bird's mouth and apply some tincture of glycerin-iodine solution (1%trypaflavine).

Trichomonas gallinae is very contagious disease and can spread through the beak (when they feed each other), food and drinking water. If the disease is recognized in time (is located only in the crop and the mouth), then immediate treatment with Dimetridazole is required.

Dimetridazole for 3-5 days or Metronidazole (Flagyl) twice daily for 5-6 days or Ronidazole for 7 days.

You must separate the infected birds from the others.

The cage and the accessories must be disinfected with hot water.

Histomoniasis

It`s caused by parasites (Histomonas meleagridis) which affect the ceca and the liver of the bird. The youngsters are more exposed to this kind of infection. Symptoms: excrements of yellow colour, walking disorders caused by the inflammation of the joints. Treatments: administration of Dimetridazole; Ronidazole; polivitamines.

It can be prevented by the disinfection of the cage or aviary through flaming and the control of humidity. Periodical disinfection of the feeding and water bowls is required and preventive administration of Dimetridazole in food is necessary. In this period is good to administer some probiotic supplements (contain beneficial bacteria) which will help to rebuild the intestinal flora of the bird. The healthy greens and veggies will also help.

Eimeria (Coccidiosis)

It`s a disease which is produced by parasites which are developing in the bird's intestinal tract. There are 9 species of Coccidia which belong to the genus Eimeria and can infect different parts of the intestine: Eimeria tenella, Eimeria acervulina, Eimeria mivati, Eimeria mitis, Eimeria necatrix, Eimeria maxima, Eimeria brunetti, Eimeria praecox,

Eimeria hagani. It could affect youngsters between 10 days and three months old.

Treatment: administration of polivitamines, sulfonamides, vitamin K, antibiotics;

Maintaining hygiene prevents diseases. Symptoms: diarrhoea with bloody mucous in it; pink intestinal tissue in droppings; lack of appetite; slow growth; anemia; etc...

The treatment is more effective if it`s done in the first days of disease. Most of the medications must be added in water. Treatments with sulfonamides will have to be associated with vitamin K3 to prevent hemorrhagic phenomenon caused by sulfaquinoxaline.

Treatments with Amprolium (Thiamine)-last for 5-7 days, they have a reduced toxicity.

It's also good to administer some polivitamines, to your birds.

Maintaining hygiene and proper food prevents diseases.

Ascariasis

It`s a parasitic disease caused by parasites (Ascaridia), which affects 3-4 months old young birds, turkeys, geese, pigeons, parrots, etc... Ascaridia galli is a white-yellowish colored worm.

Youngsters can get infected orally through infested water or feed. Massive infestation with worms could lead to the blockage of the intestine causing death if it`s not treated.

Symptoms: weakness, anorexia, diarrhoea, anaemia, hypovitaminosis, the youngsters stop developing, etc...

Treatments: piperazine salts are effective in treatments against ascariasis. Cambendazole in feed for 5 days. Fenbendazole (Panacur) in feed for 4 days. Mebendazol in feed for 7 days. Flubendazole in feed for 7 days. Disinfection of the cage or aviary through flaming and periodical disinfection of birds is required.

Toxoplasmosis

Toxoplasmosis is an infection caused by the parasite Toxoplasma gondii. Symptoms are fever, respiratory dysfunction, diarrhoea, paresis, paralysis, convulsion.

Treatments: administration of sulfonamides; antibiotics; disinfection through flaming.

It could be prevented by disinfection of cats.

Skin and feather problems

Massive molting represents the slow growth process of feathers. The affected birds have broken and disintegrated feathers.

There are multiple causes like food deficiency (the lack of amino acids, vitamins and minerals), improper maintenance (insufficient light and humidity), liver or kidney disease, tumour or hormonal disorders.

Soft molting it's a permanent or partial feather loss of the bird. The most important causes are high level of humidity, with light and food deficiency.

French molting is characterized by the continuous growth and loss of feathers without the possibility to manage to cover all parts of the bird's body. There are a few possible causes that produces the french molt, like viruses (Polyoma or Circoviruses, which have the potential to inflame feather follicles), environment changes, hereditary problems, parasites and nutrition problems. If you notice patches of bare skin on your bird's body or the molting process is not running normally, then you should visit your avian vet as soon as possible.

Inflammation of the skin (Dermatitis)

Inflammation of the skin could appear among other diseases like renal diseases with increasing level of uric acid in the blood, liver disease or infestation with external parasites.

You can use the following therapeutic measures:

-applying astringent and disinfectant solution on the wet wounds. Do not use ointments, because the feathers will become greasy and the bird can peck the wounds.

- there are injections with antibiotics which stops the bacterial infestations. Injections with multivitamins and immune system boosters can help the bird to fight against diseases.

-in case that there are itchiness problems, it would be recommended to use some special anesthetic powder for external use, on the affected areas on the skin. In this case the skin will be anaesthetised and the itchiness should disappear.

- when there are the possibility of massive bleeding (because the bird is scratching too much the affected areas) a collar should be applied around the bird's neck. In some cases the bird won't be happy to support the collar, especially if the itchiness was caused by physical problems (stress), and maybe this solution (collar) will not resolve the problem.

Xanthomas (Fatty tumors)

Xanthoma is a skin disease which affects overweight birds, especially parrots. Beneath the skin there are deposits of fatty tumors, which have yellowish color and they can be found in chest area, the wing tips, and in ventral and femoral regions (between the legs and around the vent). These encapsulated benign tumors are composed of mature fat cells. The affected areas can be easily damaged or ulcerated, especially as it gets bigger. Birds will cause self-trauma by pecking them. Xanthoma is a very common disease at birds which are fed exclusively on seeds. You'll need to introduce in the bird's diet some millet, fruits, herbs, green leafy veggies.

Once the bird get all the necessary food, the existent fatty deposits will stop developing. The eczema should be disinfected with an antiseptic solution.

Skin tumors (Lipomas)

Skin tumors can appear at all species of birds. The most common tumors are lipomas which are fatty tumors that can develop beneath the skin, and could appear on the stomach or chest area, it also can develop internally.

A common cause of lipomas is obesity and vitamin E deficiency. The proper treatment is low-fat diet. If the lipoma is big and painful or infected your vet will surgically remove the tumor, because this is the best option for your bird's health.

The appetite and the digestive system

The bird doesn't want to eat and drink

If your bird refuse to eat and drink, then its life is in danger. The loss of appetite indicate an illness of internal organs, which could be very dangerous. In this case you'll need to contact your avian vet as soon as possible.

The bird eats too much

Some birds have very big appetite, but they'll remain still skinny, because they suffer from parasitic infestation with acarians - Dermanyssus gallinae.

In this situation you'll have to clean the cage or aviary and the bird's internal and external disinfection is required.

You need to offer them some hemp and poppy seeds, and iron sulphate in water.

When the bird has diarrhoea

When a bird has diarrhoea, the droppings are very soft even fluids, with a smell different from normal. The frequency of elimination of droppings will be very high.

Diarrhoea leads to dehydration of the bird and to loss of minerals of the organism. There are multiple causes:

- inadequate nutrition (bad quality)
- bacterial infection of the intestines
- intoxications
- parasites

The required treatment is focused on antidiarrheal diet and specific medication for each situation.

You will need to feed your bird with some poppy seeds, because of their calming effect; boiled rice; some fried seeds and replace water with mint tea. You can add to mashed boiled rice some coal powder.

Antidiarrheal medication will be followed after your avian vet advice. You can also offer to your bird instead of water a special solution which contains minerals and it could be prepared at pharmacies:

NaCl (sodium chloride)	8.0 g
CaCl2 (calcium chloride)	0.13 g
KCl (potassium chloride)	0.2 g
MgCl (magnesium chloride)	0.1 g
NaH2PO4 (monosodium phosphate)	0.05 g
NaHCO3 (sodium bicarbonate)	10 g
Glucose	1.0 g
Distilled water	1000.0 ml

It`s very important to separate your bird from the others, to assure an adequate temperature of the room 77 - 95 degrees Fahrenheit (25 - 35 degrees Celsius) and a very strict hygiene.

Enteritis (Inflammation of the intestines)

Enteritis represent the inflammation of the intestines and it`s one of the most frequent cause of mortality at cage and aviary birds.

The main causes of enteritis are:

Nutrition

Bad quality food; inadequate composition of the food;

Intoxications

Toxic plants, lead, etc...

Intestinal parasites

Tapeworms, eelworms, coccidia can harm the intestinal mucus;

Viruses

There are different kind of viruses: Paramyxoviruses and hepatitis viruses, which can also cause enteritis;

Bacterial infections

Salmonellosis and E. coli are pathogenic bacterias which are the main causes of the enteritis. The main symptom of the enteritis is diarrhoea. The feathers around the cloaca are dirty, the bird is lethargic, sad and sleeps too much. Because it has lost too much liquid, the affected bird will drink much water. Laboratory investigations (bacteriological and parasitological analyses) will have to be done to discover the main cause of the enteritis.

Meanwhile, the bird has to be placed in a warm place, it will need infusions and forced feeding. Injection with vitamins will strengthen the immune system of the bird. The avian vet will prescribe the proper antibiotics treatments for your bird.

Gastrointestinal parasites - Tapeworms

Tapeworms which lives in the bird's body, eliminate their eggs through the bird's feces.

The eggs are consumed by intermediate hosts (earthworms, snails and insects like grasshoppers, ants, beetles, flies, etc...). Inside of the intermediate hosts a small embryo develops in the eggs but does not hatch immediately.

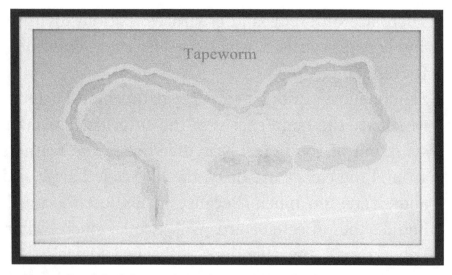

When the bird is eating the infected insects or worms the larvae in the egg reaches infective stage within two to three weeks and they will become tapeworms in the bird's body. The eggs are consumed by intermediate hosts (earthworms, snails and insects like grasshoppers, ants, beetles, flies, etc...).

Wild parrots are infested with tapeworms when they eat insects and worms directly from the wild. Wild parrots which were recently imported (captured from the wild) may have a prophylactic treatment against the tapeworm with Praziquantel. Infestation with tapeworms is uncommon in domestically raised parrots.

Capillaria (Capillary or Threadworms)

There are several species of Capillaria and can be found in the lower intestinal tract causing severe inflammation of it. Disinfection of the cage and accessories is required with hot water and treatments with Hygromycin may be used.

Constipation

The signs of constipation are the enlarged abdomen of the bird, and the missing fresh droppings on the cage floor. The impossibility of elimination of droppings leads to intoxication. The general state of the bird is getting worse, it will have slovenly aspect.

In this situation, the cloacal orifice free opening is needed by administering few drops of castor oil through the bird's beak, for two-three days. The bird will need a warm place and for the next few days the diet will contain honey, green plants and fruits.

Obesity

Obesity could lead to health problems like heart and circulatory system disorders, joints problems, modification of the internal organs like liver fattening and constipation. The major problems are the impossibility of flying, loneliness, and overfeeding with flax and rape seeds.

The main measures that must be taken are the introduction of lettuce in the bird's diet and increase the frequency of free flight in the room. You can replace the drinking water with dandelion tea, for 20 days. The obese bird will have to receive only half part of the usual daily seeds portion. Green food and fruits can be offered daily.

Excessive weight loss

The excessive weight loss of the bird could have multiple causes like nutritional and parasitic problems. The suffering bird has dry skin and a very prominent breastbone.

When you observe these symptoms, you'll have to disinfect the cage and the bird, and get droppings samples for further examinations. Your avian vet will inform you with a right diagnose and will establish the treatment.

Inflammation of the crop

The inflammation of the crop usually appears because of bacterial, fungal or parasitic infections. The dirty drinking water from the bowls can be the cause of the infection. If the water bowls are not cleaned at least once per day with hot water, then toxic mosses and dirt could form in the recipients. The affected bird is vomiting and the feathers on the bird's head are dirty and sticky. The affected bird could also suffer from diarrhoea and became very somnolent and lethargic. You'll have to increase the body temperature of the bird with a heating lamp. The avian vet will prescribe anti inflammatory medication which has to be administered through the beak. Before the treatment with antibiotics laboratory investigations should be made for a precise diagnosis. In this period the affected bird diet is based on soft food: boiled eggs, biscuit soaked in water, boiled rice, etc... If the bird doesn't want to eat, you'll have to force feed it. Even if the bird has recovered you'll have to take care of him/her a few weeks after, otherwise it will get sick again. You can warm up the bird when it's needed and injection with vitamin A is required.

Liver diseases

Inflammation of the liver (Hepatitis)

The affected birds look tired, lethargic and with lack of appetite. The affected liver is not able to help much the body with detoxification. Most birds suffer from itching, and feather plucking. Because of the inflammation of the liver, on the bird's skin can appear some inflammation, the urine color is white and the feces are greenish-yellow. The main factors that triggers acute chronic hepatic inflammations are bacterias, viruses, funguses, parasites or intoxications. The liver is increasing in size, but it`s an organ with incredible regeneration power if the disease is discovered in time. If the hepatic tissue is very affected, then it can't regenerate and we talk about cirrhosis of the liver. The therapy of the cirrhosis is impossible. The evolution of it can be stopped when it is recognized in time. Treatments with liver protection medication could be done. The possible cause could be the perishable oily seeds. Hazelnut mould (Aspergillus flavus) which is forming in wet weather on the nutshell, are extremely toxic for the liver. You'll have to check the quality of the nuts before you offer it to your bird, by tasting them. Try to use brands that are sold with success in stores and supermarkets, this way you'll have the chance to buy fresh nuts.

Fatty liver

It`s a disease which appears especially at overweight birds. The accumulation of fat excess in the liver cells makes the liver to work improperly. The main symptoms are: diarrhoea and respiratory difficulties; the nails and the beak is overgrown. When the liver increases too much in size, the tissue of the liver could break up and internal bleeding could appear, causing death. To avoid these kind of situations, slow weight loss is needed, by reducing the consume of oily seeds, administration of vitamin E and liver protection medication and lots of exercise is recommended (outdoor flying) to regenerate the liver function.

Beak health problems

Deformed beak

When the owners don't offer cuttlefish bone to their birds, then their beak will overgrow, which will lead to the impossibility of the bird to feed and drink. If the beak it`s not cut back in appropriate time, the bird could die, due to impossibility to feed itself. When the bird feeds mostly soft food instead of seeds, then it doesn`t use sufficiently the upper and lower parts of it`s beak. You'll have to replace the soft food with the right diet and offer some tree branches to your bird to chew. Some owners use to cut their parrot's beak even if it`s unnecessary, this way they will accelerate the growing process of the beak. The abnormal growth of the beak, in some cases, could be because of a serious health disorder.

Soft beak

The beak of some birds becomes very flexible because of the vitamins and calcium deficiency. In this case, the bird will need soft food, you'll have to grease the bird's beak with vitamin A and some calcium and crushed egg shells administration is required. The main cause is vitamins A, C, biotin, pantothenic acid, folic acid and calcium or phosphorus deficiency. Sometimes on the beak could appear some exfoliation which looks like scales. You must grease the beak with cod-liver oil or with vitamin A.

Injuries of the beak

At birds which suffer from malformed beak, because of vitamins and calcium or phosphorus deficiency, the beak could break very easily even when the bird try to break the nutshells.

Administration of soft food, fruits, calcium is required, vitamin A application on the beak with a piece of cotton - wool, and a professional remediation of the broken beak made by an avian vet will give good results. But injuries of the beak could happen because of the accidents. There are several ways to reconstitute malformed or injured beaks. Prosthetic beaks are made by inserting pins into the bone of the existing beak which is then covered by a dental acrylic material and shaped.

Respiratory system problems

The loud whistling sounds and hard breathing of the bird indicates a problem with it`s respiratory system. The birds are very sensitive at air currents and they get cold very easy. To prevent these kind of problems, you'll need to find a proper place for the cage. When you hear this whistling noises, you must feed the bird with grated carrots and fruits and green plants rich in vitamin C.

The avian vet help is needed to prescribe the right antibiotics for the bird.

Another respiratory problem is, when the bird is breathing with the open beak. In this case the bird`s tracheas are infested with a parasitic worm, called Syngamus trachealis.

Acute respiratory insufficiency

Respiratory insufficiency is a symptom which usually appears at many and different kind of health disorders. Respiratory difficulties can develop after the modification of the internal organs which are pressing the air ways. When the thyroid gland increases in size, it can restrain the air ways. All the internal organs are situated in the same cavity of the body (thoracic cavity and the stomach are not separated by a diaphragm as at mammals), and the modification of the internal organs may influence negatively the respiratory functions. The normal function of the air sacs and the lungs is affected by the increase of the liver, by obesity, sexual disorders and accumulation of excrements as a result of digestive diseases. When it's a slow evolution process of the disease, the affected bird is flying less, not singing and sleeps too much. After all, the bird will lose its strength, yawns very often, because of the lack of oxygen. The affected bird is breathing rapidly with open beak. If the bird is not taken in time to the vet for consultation and treatment, the bird could suffocate.

Abundant nose secretions

The secretion which appears at nose area indicates that the bird is cold sick. You can maintain the bird's body temperature by covering it with a piece of cotton cloth.

There are lots of secretions in the nose when the bird is suffering from mycotic, bacterial and viral infestations.

You have to avoid the contact of your bird with other wild birds and you must feed the bird with soft food, seeds soaked in milk, honey and chamomile tea. Vitamins A, C, and B complex intake is needed.

Rhinitis

Rhinitis is an inflammation of the nostrils. The feathers around the nostrils are dirty, because of the abundant nose secretion. The nasal discharge can form a crust and can block the nasal orifices. The bird rubs his head on perches and on different objects of the cage to liberate his/her affected nostrils. The main cause of rhinitis is infection with viruses, bacterias or mycoplasmosis. Rhinitis is transmissible from parrot to human. For this reason, the avian vet will administer an injection with antibiotic (Tetracycline). In case that the infection is resistant to Tetracycline, laboratory investigation is needed to find the proper antibiotic for the bird. Injections with Poly Vitamins are also indicated and vitamin C (powder), (a pinch of vitamin C powder in 30 ml of water) added in drinking water to fight the infection. The nostrils and the feathers around it will have to be cleaned with cotton wool soaked in warm water, few times per day. The inflamed and red skin around the nostrils have to be greased with a special ointment, which contains fish grease, marigold (Calendula officinalis) and vitamin A. Because the body temperature of the bird drops, you'll have to warm it up, by placing a heat lamp or bulb (60-100W) near the cage. The "warming up " procedure has to be done until the bird is recovering. You can also place a bowl filled with hot chamomile infusion in front of the cage. You'll have to cover the cage with a towel and try to direct the hot streams inside the cage. You can apply this method once or twice per day. Disinfection with hot water of the perches, feeding and drinking bowls is required. Rhinitis could affect those birds which lives in preheated rooms, especially during winter. Because of the dry air, the bird`s airways become affected. To control the humidity of the room, you can place a wet towel on the radiator. There are also special humidifying equipments or you may also offer your bird the opportunity to have baths every day. You can also spray your bird daily with warm water.

Sense organs problems

The eyes

The bird's eyes problems could have noninfectious and infectious causes. Non infectious diseases are swollen eyelids (blepharitis), glaucoma, conjunctivitis, cataracts and traumas.

Infectious eye diseases could appear in ornithosis, avian mycoplasmosis or chlamydiosis.

Non infectious eye problems could be treated with vitamin A (drops) applied on the eyes with cotton buds. You can also clean the eyes with chamomile tea.

The ears

There are rare cases of ears infections at birds. Usually, the bird is continuously scratching the infected ear, which means that the interior area is inflamed. The bird frequently shake its head and hold its head on one side. You'll have to apply in each ear one drop of boroglycerine. If the symptoms still persist, then visit your avian vet for antibiotic prescription.

Reproduction problems

The retention of the egg

A frequent problem at cage birds is the retention of the egg. If the hen can`t lay the egg, it could over press the internal organs. The impossibility to eliminate droppings, could lead to self intoxication. It can happen because of the age of the bird, the size and shape of the egg, the sudden drops of temperature 53.6 degrees Fahrenheit (12 degrees Celsius) and the stress during the egg laying process. At the first signs of the retention of the egg, the wet heat will help in most of the cases. You'll have to place a bowl filled with hot water in front of the cage, which must be covered with a towel and the hot steams have to be directed towards the cage. A heating lamp or bulb (60 W) will be necessary near the cage and directed towards the suffering bird. You can also help your bird by introducing 0.5-1 ml of warm oil in the cloacal orifice. This operation should continue each hour until the egg is delivered. In this case, for the bird`s safe, the vet intervention is required.

The temperature in the room has to be maintained around 86 degrees Fahrenheit (30 degrees Celsius).

Infertility of the cock

One of the main cause of the infertility of the cock is the unsuitable partner and for this reason the birds need to be watched during mating period. The stress, inadequate feeding, too young and too old age of the birds could be the reason of the infertility.

During mating period, the cock`s diet should increase with vitamin E.

Nervous system problems

Dizzy bird

The bird can't hold itself on the perch and could fall and hurt itself, causing serious injuries.

During the flight they can't appreciate the right distance. To avoid accidents, the floor of the cage must be covered with a thin piece of cloth. The free flight must be stopped until the clarification of the causes.

Twirling or Torticollis

They constantly throw their head back, walk around in circle, turn their head around in a circle and look up. If there is cerebral diseases, then the bird need to stay in a dark and quiet place on a piece of soft cloth. There could be several causes:

- infections with viruses, bacteria, parasites, mycoplasma- administration of antibiotics is needed
- intoxication with lead, insecticides - administration of antidote is required
- injuries and brain hemorrhage
- avitaminosis A and lack of calcium - administration of necessary substances
- brain tumors

Diseases of the feet

Abscess of the feet

The main causes of this disease are the circulatory disorders of the feet caused by insufficient movement, inappropriate perches, avitaminosis A (too little green food and fruits). First the abscess forms on the heel or under a toe (a pressure zone). The skin become very thin, the wound appears and soon it will be covered with crust. The affected feet is swollen and it`s very warm. The wound become an open injury filled with pus. The crust has to be removed surgically and the affected foot will be treated with medicated ointment. The affected bird will be supervised for 10 days. The bandage has to be changed at every 2-3 days. Injection with multivitamins stimulates the healing process. To spare the other foot, the perches must be wrapped with paper towel or with bandages and they have to be fixed at the end of perches with adhesive tape. All the perches available in the cage have to be wrapped, because the bird will hesitate to sit on them. If there are not pustules filled with pus on the bird's foot, it's enough to use ointment with vitamin A or with fish fat (grease) daily. During this treatment the presence of the grit is not necessary in the cage, because it will stick on the bird`s foot and it will stop the healing process.

Offer your bird the opportunity to free-flight every day for 1-2 hours. This way the circulatory system and the blood circulation in the feet will be stimulated. The lack of movement and the overweight body of the bird has negative effects on the feet.

Accidents and injuries of the limb

Sprains and dislocations

Sprains appears after the wrong manipulation of the bird or its leg is stuck between the bars.

The affected joints are inflamed causing pain and the affected area is increasing in size. In the case of sprains, the treatment consists in application of a bandage with wool balls soaked in alcohol and the settlement of the bird in quiet place is required.

In the case of a dislocation, re-suspend the ends of joints in the initial position and then maintain them in this position by applying around the hip joint an adhesive tape.

You can feed your bird with poppy and hemp seeds, and an everyday observation of the bird is required.

Fractures

Fractures appear as a result of accidents through manipulation or bumping of the bird.

The leg is dragged and the opposite extremity of the fracture moves. The affected area is turgid, much bigger, infiltrated with blood and lymph. If the fracture is open, then it can be observed the rupture of the muscle and skin, with the visibility of the bones.

The stages of the treatment are:

-the treatment has to be done in maximum 48 hours from the accident

- calming the pain with infiltration of pain killer
- disinfection of the area with ethacridine lactate (Rivanol solution)
- removal of the impurities
- immobilization of the area
- attach a collar around the bird's head to prevent tearing the bandage
- administration of antibiotics and vitamins, daily
- supervision of the evolution of the fracture

The advantage of surgical operation compared with traditional method is that the fracture can be more perfectly remediate.

Gout

When uric acid level becomes too high in the bird's blood stream, then gout occurs. Birds usually don't produce too much urine. The uric acid is removed from the blood by the kidneys and eliminated through the urine. When the kidneys don't work properly, the level of uric acid becomes too high in the blood stream and it will become crystallized. In articular gout the uric acid crystallizes in the joints, ligaments and tendon sheaths, forming white nodules which could be very painful. The feet are swollen and become red-violet color. When the uric acid crystallizes in tissues, it will form small, white nodules. In visceral gout, uric acid deposits are found in the liver, kidneys, spleen and air sacs. High dose of vitamin A, lots of fluids may be given and stimulation of renal function by adding in drinking water sucrose (sugar) could positively influence the evolution of disease. Because of the swollen feet and painful nodules the bird may be unable to perch and so it will remain on the floor of the cage. The food and water bowls should be placed to be easily accessible locations, by helping the bird to be able to eat and drink without any problem. The perches have to be wrapped with paper towels and the cage has to contain little wrapped platforms to help the bird to sit comfortable.

Nodules could be eliminated surgically when they have a specific size. In this case it`s not recommended anesthesia, because it could harm the affected kidneys.

Intoxications of the cage birds

Intoxication with: - disinfection substances: the bird has difficulty in breathing, it has discoloured eyes. The bird's life is in danger!

 -soap or deodorants: they contain a substance which could lead to temporary blindness. Washing the affected area with cold water.

- **alcohol:** the bird is vomiting, it has fluffy feathers, stays in the corner of the cage, it`s losing balance. The sick and old birds could die; the healthy bird could recover by itself.

-**toxic plants:** digestive symptoms, diarrhoea. You need to assure green plants in your bird's diet.

-**nicotine (cigarette buts):** it can affect the nervous system, causing death. Don't leave cigarettes near the birds.

-**salt (and salty food):** the bird is very thirsty, it is agitated and shaking. You'll need to administrate lots of water through the bird's beak; laxatives; in severe situations, the bird could die.

-**teflon (from frying pans):** suffocation and death in 30 minutes. Avoid keeping the
bird in the kitchen; in case of accidents remove the bird outside as fast as possible.

-**lead (newspapers, lead-based paint):** green coloured diarrhoea (even the presence of blood), the kidneys, the bone's marrow and the nervous system are affected. If the accident is discovered in time, the administration of an antidot is required - calcium EDTA (aminopolycarboxylic acid).
The major intoxications take place when the birds, swallow the toxic substances. The owner could offer some milk with a dropper and after that, the bird will start vomiting in short time.

Another solution is the administration of medicinal coal. You'll have to dissolve 5 grams of medicinal coal in 50 ml of water. This preparation will need to be administered through the beak. Once you have made the operations described above, after one hour, you'll have to administer some oily purgatives, oil or castor oil.

Bird diseases which could affect humans

Allergies of humans at fluffs and feathers: the affected persons are sneezing, on the skin they present eruptions or bouts of asthma; it triggers allergic sinusitis. You'll have to avoid birds breeding.

Tuberculosis (mycobacterium avium): it's very rare at humans. Healthy people usually do not contact the disease from the birds, just those with immunodeficiency. Tuberculosis is a treatable disease at humans. It could affect the birds (very rare), it has bad general condition, weakness, nodules on organs.

Ornithosis; Psittacosis; Chlamydiosis; Chlamydia Psittaci: it is transmissible through the air, it`s like influenza with 104 degrees Fahrenheit(40 degrees Celsius) fever, the incubation period is 10 days. It could be treated with antibiotics at humans.

The symptoms at affected birds are fever, somnolence, breathing problems and diarrhoea. It can be treated with antibiotics at birds as well.

Viruses;Orthomyxoviruses; Paramyxoviruses: the Orthomyxoviruses are the symptoms of influenza; Paramyxoviruses are the cause of conjunctivitis and signs of flu. The treatment at humans is made by supporting the body functions with the appropriate medication.

At birds the symptoms are: bird pest caused by Orthomyxoviruses; and nervous symptoms caused by Paramyxoviruses. The treatment at birds is made by a specialised avian vet.

Bacteriosis (Salmonella, Klebsiella Pneumoniae): digestive problems at humans. The treatment consist in administration of antibiotics after a laboratory examination.

At birds there are digestive problems as well. The administration of antibiotics is required, after a laboratory examination.

Contagious diseases at birds

Contagious diseases could be transmitted through different ways from one bird to another or from birds to other animals.

The contagious diseases are manifested by fever, behavioral, posture changes.

Prevention of diseases

It's more important to prevent the disease than to treat it. When you notice that your bird doesn't eat well, has diarrhoea, there`s unusual secretion in the nose, it`s sleepy, then isolate it and visit your avian vet as soon as possible. The cage, the drinking and bathing bowls and the perches will need to be cleaned and disinfected with special products recommended by your vet. When you bring a new bird in the house, you'll have to quarantine it for two weeks, to be sure that the " new bird" is totally healthy.

Viral diseases

Viruses are in a continuous transformation, and the birds with other animals, constitute a reservoir of viruses. There are several vaccines for birds, which helps them to fight against the viruses.The treatment of viral diseases is based on the support of vital functions of bird and the capacity to fight viruses. Administration of vitamins, good quality food and antibiotics (at the recommendation of the avian vet).

Avian pseudo pest (Newcastle disease)

The avian pseudo pest is a very contagious disease which mostly affects the backyard birds and could contaminate the cage birds as well. The spread of the pseudo pest virus is made by already infested wild birds (sparrows, crows, magpies). It could be spread through food, water and air. The cage birds are usually placed near the infested backyard birds, which is wrong. Infested birds have several symptoms like diarrhoea with or without blood, dehydration, loss of weight, breathing difficulties, discharges from nostrils, fever, paralysis of the legs and wings, anorexia, indigestion, torticollis. Disinfection of the cage or aviary is required. Vaccination of the bird is made which must be given subcutaneously or intramuscularly. If the vaccine is administered in water, you'll have to be sure that the water, the water recipients and the cage are perfectly clean.

Avian pox at cage birds

The Avipox virus could affect every backyard and aviary bird. It`s also called "the suffocation disease". The signs of this disease is: breathing through open beak, conjunctivitis and catarrh. There is a cutaneous form which appears as yellowish nodules, on the eyelids, around the nose, cloaca and inside face of the wings. The evolution is very fast at youngsters, without any signs of disease. The virus can be transmitted by direct contact with infected chickens or by mosquitoes. Administration of vaccine is required which has to be given every year. Avipoxvirus is very resistant in the dark and can survive 14 days at 38 degrees Celsius (100,4 degrees Fahrenheit), 15 months at room temperature and 5 minutes at 100 degrees Celsius (212 degrees Fahrenheit). It can be destroyed with caustic soda 1-2%. There are at least 3 different types of Avipox Viruses: fowlpox viruses (chickens, turkeys, peacocks, pheasants); pigeon poxviruses and canarypox viruses (canaries, sparrows). The disease can be transmitted directly or indirectly from sick birds: sparrows, crows, owls, seagulls; from insects: mosquitoes, flies, ticks, (the virus can resist in these insects bodies for 90-100 days); and by contaminated water, feed, beddings. The period of incubation is 3-15 days. In cutaneous localization the disease is characterized by the appearance of the nodules around the beak, eye lids, feet which at first have white - yellowish color, then become brown.

Localization of the nodules on the mucus of membranes (diphtheritic) is manifesting by the appearance of the different shapes of the false membranes affecting the upper respiratory system and digestive system. When the diphtheria lesions affects the larynx and trachea, the birds could die through asphyxiation. Mixed localizations are characterized by the appearance of the nodules (cutaneous form) and of the false membranes on the mucus.

Pacheco's disease

It`s caused by a group of psittacine herpesviruses, a highly contagious disease, with incubation period of 3-14 days, causing sudden death. The infested bird has lack of appetite, diarrhoea, white-yellowish droppings with blood in it. Sometimes they present conjunctivitis, sinusitis and loss of balance. The sick bird has balance disorder and can`t hold itself on the perch. An antiviral drug (Acyclovir) followed by supportive treatments can reduce death rates in other exposed birds.

Marek`s disease

It`s an infectious disease caused by a virus from Herpesviridae family, which resists 7 days in feces, up to 16 weeks in beddings and 6 weeks in dust particles. Marek`s disease is a type of avian cancer which most commonly affects the backyard birds. Tumors can occur in the eyes and cause irregularly shaped pupils and blindness. Tumors of the kidneys, liver, pancreas, muscles can cause incoordination, paleness and weak labored breathing. The birds can be vaccinated against tumor formation, but does not prevent the infection with the virus. The Marek's virus is transmitted by the air and it also affects the respiratory and digestive system. Marek`s disease appears in multiple forms:

Neural localization is manifesting with lack of balance, paralyses of the feet, wings and neck. If the cranial nerves are affected, then the neck is contorted, the affected bird can't walk or feed properly and it could die after 30-60 days. Ocular localization could be found at adult birds and it's manifesting by ocular disorders, discoloration of the iris like silvery-blue and irregular shaped pupils. These modifications lead to impossibility of feeding, weight loss, dehydration and death.

Visceral localization is characterized by anemia, diarrhoea, deformation of the abdomen.

Cutaneous localization appears at youngsters, there are deformities at the feather follicles and appears like large nodules or crusty looking lesions.

Acute form also affects youngsters and the signs are: weakness,refuse of food, paralysis. Decontamination of the cage or aviary is required.

Diagnosis: differentiate from botulism; calcium / phosphorus /vitamin D deficiency; lymphoid leukosis, etc... Birds exposed to Marek's disease are considered carriers for life, even if they were previously vaccinated.

Bacterial diseases

Avian respiratory mycoplasmosis

It`s a chronic infectious disease which can be found at chickens, turkeys, pheasants, quails, peacocks, etc... At youngsters of 2-3 days old the symptoms are characterized by respiratory problems and conjunctivitis and it has a slow evolution. At adult birds is characterized by weight loss, respiratory disorders. The wild birds are the cause of infection. The affected adult birds can transmit the infection through their eggs.

Symptoms at youngsters: stagnation in developing, sneeze and cough, open beak breathing, sinusitis, enteritis, lack of appetite, respiratory disorders. Confirmation of disease is made after a laboratory examination. Prevention consists in disinfection of the cage or aviary and preventive treatments of youngsters with antibiotics. To combat mycoplasmosis, the sick birds have to be isolated and those which are apparently healthy, have to be preventively treated with antibiotics. Terramycin administered subcutaneously in superior part of the neck. After the administration of injection with

Terramycin it will appear a local reaction which will usually disappear after 10-14 days.

It is also recommended Oxytetracycline or Streptomycin for 3 days or Erythromycin intramuscularly for 5-7 days. Administration of vitamins in drinking water or feed is also recommended.

Pasteurellosis

It`s an infection caused by a bacteria called Pasteurella which is found in humans and animals as well. The infection could spread through droppings and saliva of animals. It affects mostly adult birds and the symptoms are fever, tiredness, and the presence of mucous in droppings.

Treatment: Chloramphenicol; Oxytetracycline; Tetracycline;

Salmonellosis is produced by a bacteria which affects all species of birds. It cause digestive disorders, fever, diarrhoea, conjunctivitis and damage of the internal organs. Salmonellosis could spread through contaminated drinking water and food. The treatment includes Oxytetracycline hydrochloride; Tetracycline in water or food; Chloramphenicol in food (if the bird accept it).

Pullorum and Salmonella gallinarum affects young birds between 1-21 days, and it has a

high rate of mortality. Symptoms are white droppings and lack of appetite.

Treatments: Chloramphenicol, injectable.

Psittacosis or parrot fever

It`s caused by a bacteria called Chlamydia psittaci and it can be identified at more than 130 species of birds: parrots, canaries, pigeons, geese, ducks, turkeys, chickens, pheasants, doves, seagulls, etc... Symptoms are: lack of appetite, weight loss, tiredness, conjunctivitis, fever, respiratory disorders, white-green or bloody colored diarrhoea. It is transmitted directly from bird to bird or by infested sand, fluff and droppings. The sick bird may shiver, it's lethargic and present discharge from the nose and eyes. Before the administration of the antibiotics, laboratory analysis of the droppings and blood sample will be necessary for a precise diagnosis.

To combat disease separate the sick birds from healthy ones and disinfect the cage. You must use protection equipment to avoid infestation. After this process the protection equipments have to be sterilized. The affected birds have to be treated with Tetracycline or Doxycycline for 3 weeks. At humans the symptoms are as like flu with a strong pneumonia.

Mycotic diseases

Mycotic diseases start with indisposed state, lack of appetite, weight loss, less singing, digestive problems. Moulds produces mycotoxins which attacks the liver and kidneys.

Candida (Candidiasis)

Candida is an infection with the yeast Candida albicans, which is normally present in low numbers in the bird's digestive system. If the yeast increase in the digestive tract, Candida could cause problems in other organs like the beak and respiratory system. Candida could also infect the skin, eyes and the reproductive tract of the bird. Infestation of young birds could happen very easily.

Treatments: Stamycin diluted in water and administered through the beak.

Aspergillosis

Aspergillosis is a respiratory disease, caused by infection with a fungus, called Aspergillus. Damp bedding and food, inadequate cage cleaning, humidity can increase the number of fungal spores which are inhaled from the environment. Aspergillosis develops in lungs and air sacs of the bird. Open mouthed breathing and respiratory signs are increasing severity of disease.

Treatment: Stamycin in drinking water; potassium iodide in drinking water.

Aviary plants and shrubs

Here are a few plants and shrubs that will delight your birds, but remember any plant can cause harm if your bird consumes a large enough amount of it.

Blackberry (Rubus fruticosus)

Birch (Betula spp.)

Marigold (Calendula officinalis)

Lemon balm (Melissa officinalis)

Elderberry (Sambucus nigra): in Autumn the berries will grow almost anywhere;

Snowberry (Symphoricarpos albus): the birds will find this plant fascinating;

Dog Rose (Rosa canina): it has scarlet hips and beautiful flowers;

Hawthorn (Crataegus monogyna): it is ideal for nesting;

Delphinium: the birds will enjoy the seeds of this plant;

Valerian (Centranthus ruber): can be planted anywhere, the roots have restraint effect on rats;

Sunflower (Helianthus multiflorus): can be planted anywhere;

Tree Mallow (Lavatera olbia): it has red flowers which grow up in July and August;

Holly (Ilex aquifolium): birds will love this plant;

Oregon Grape (Mahonia aquifolium): that shrub will survive most ravages or soils.

Jasmine (Jasminum officinale): there are Summer and Winter varieties which will produce yellow or white flowers;

Plants that could cause intoxication to your parrots

Rhododendron, Flamingo Flower, Snowdrop (Galanthus nivalis), Geranium or Stork's bills (Pelargonium), Bearberry (Rhamnus purshiana), Ivy (Hedera helix), Lesser celandine (Ranunculus ficaria), Deadly nightshade (Atropa belladonna), Tobacco (Nicotiana tabacum), mistletoe (Viscum album), Philodendron (Monstera deliciosa), Wood spurge (Euphorbia amygdaloides), Autumn crocus (Colchicum autumnale), Avocado (Persea americana), Peach (Prunus persica), Tomato (Lycopersicon esculentum).

Disclaimer

The author accepts no responsibility for any loss or injury, as a result for the use or misuse of the information in this book.

You should always ask for a qualified advice from your avian vet, before you plan using any medication especially antibiotics. Always check and double check the prescription that should come along with the medication you intend to use for your birds. I hope this book will help you keep your birds happy and healthy and it is been a pleasure for me to write it down for you. Please check the following page where you can find my other writings:

More from the author

1.Citron - Crested Cockatoos: All About Nutrition, Training, Care, Diseases And Treatments

2.Bird Care: Keeping Happy And Healthy Citron - Crested Cockatoos

3.Bird Care: Citron - Crested Cockatoos: Diseases and Treatments

4.Senegal parrots: All About Nutrition, Training, Care, Diseases And Treatments

16. Bird Care Zebra Finches: Diseases & Treatments

17. Natural Remedies - How to prevent and cure any diseases with plants from A-Z

18.Cooking for parrots

19.Cockatiels: All About Nutrition, Training, Care, Diseases And Treatments

20.Bird Care: Keeping Healthy And Happy Cockatiels

21.Bird Care: Cockatiels: Diseases and Treatments

You can find all these books on Amazon.com.

Brought to you by Erika Busecan

CPSIA information can be obtained
at www.ICGtesting.com
Printed in the USA
LVHW04s1245190518
577799LV00024B/216/P